Spiritual Dimensions
of
Psychology

Volumes now available in the series
The Collected Works of Hazrat Inayat Khan:

Personality: The Art of Being and Becoming
The Awakening of the Human Spirit
Spiritual Dimensions of Psychology
The Bowl of Saki
Gayan, Vadan, Nirtan
Tales Told by Hazrat Inayat Khan
Nature Meditations
The Unity of Religious Ideals
Mastery Through Accomplishment
The Soul Whence and Whither
The Complete Sayings of Hazrat Inayat Khan

Spiritual Dimensions
of
Psychology

HAZRAT INAYAT KHAN

Sufi Order Publications

For Information Contact:
THE SUFI ORDER
P.O. Box 574
Lebanon Springs, N.Y. 12114
(518) 794-8181

Second printing, July 1982

Spiritual Dimensions of Psychology
© 1981 by Sufi Order. All rights reserved.

SUFI ORDER PUBLICATIONS
1570 Pacheco Street
Sante Fe, New Mexico 87501

Library of Congress Catalog Card No. 80-54830

Printed in the United States of America
ISBN 0-930872-24-X

EDITOR'S NOTE

This compilation of Hazrat Inayat Khan's teachings on psychology is made up of transcripts of lectures the Sufi master gave in the 1910s and twenties. Some of this material has previously been published, scattered throughout a number of volumes in the "Sufi Message" series; a large portion of it, including most of the papers in Part Four, on psychic power and the higher vision, has never before been made public.

Since *Spiritual Dimensions of Psychology* consists of individual lectures, there is an occasional overlap of subject matter from one chapter to another, and the reader is therefore urged to make use of the index. A number of passages have been deleted and the sequence of others slightly modified to facilitate the flow of ideas and to eliminate as much repetition as possible.

Psychology is a vast area, and in its broadest sense—the nature and perfectability of the human being—it is the basis of much of Hazrat Inayat Khan's work. Further aspects of the subject will be treated in forthcoming volumes in *The Collected Works of Hazrat Inayat Khan*.

I would like to express my deep gratitude to Pir Vilayat Inayat Khan and to Sajjada and Sikander Kopelman for their inspiration and guidance in the preparation of this book. Thanks are also due to Zahira Rabinowitz and to Munir and Farida Graham for their generous help with proofreading and indexing.

—Anka Laura de la Torre Bueno

TABLE OF CONTENTS

Editor's Note v
Introduction by Pir Vilayat Inayat Khan ix

Part One: Psychology: The Science of Mind 1

1. Psychology, Science, and Esotericism 3
2. Mind and Body 8
3. Mental Creation 10
4. Divine Mind 16

Part Two: The Nature of the Mind 23

5. Thought and Imagination 25
6. Suggestion 32
    Impression and Belief 37
    Word and Voice 45
    Movement 49
    Suggestion in Practice 55
7. Reflection 58
    Man and Animals 58
    Communication and Obsession 63
    Repetition 67
    The Expansion of the Heart 69
8. Reason 75
9. Memory 82
10. The Heart 88

Part Three: Training the Mind 93

11. Will Power 95
     Developing the Will 99
12. Concentration 105
     Mystical Concentration 109
13. Mental Purification 124
     Stilling the Mind 124
     Breath.....................................129
     Attitude 138
14. Unlearning 145
15. The Pure Mind 151

Part Four: The Mind of the Seer 157

16. Psychic Power 159
     The Development of Psychic Power 164
     The Use of Psychic Power......................166
17. Insight 172
     The Vision of the Seer 174
     The Development of Insight 178
18. Impression 185
     The Mental Record...........................187
     Expression..................................192
19. Intuition...................................202
20. Inspiration 207
21. Dream.....................................213
     The Types of Dream...........................217
22. Vision 222
23. Revelation..................................229
     Index......................................235

INTRODUCTION
by
Pir Vilayat Inayat Khan

For the Sufi, the mind is a world of its own: a palace of mutually reflecting mirrors, in which imagination emerges creatively out of the divine mind—or sometimes runs riot. It is a self-creative realm, where everything thought acquires an existence having its own laws, irrespective of the physical universe. Here memories mesh with memories, moving out of their time-bound setting into the timeless. Here inventions outreach their utility, and ideas interface and cross-pollenate, averring themselves to be anonymous.

Like his Sufi predecessors, Hazrat Inayat Khan sees the divine hand in every happening and every thought. Behind what we think is our individual thinking, he sees the thinking of humanity as a whole; if you like, the thinking of the planet: planetary consciousness, which is an extension of the divine mind. For what we believe are our consciousnesses are an infinite array of mirrors, reflecting the One in manifold forms. Indeed, creativity is tapping the divine thinking. It is the mirror's impurities that distort, causing the world of maya, imagination run amok. We recognize here our world of incessant fantasies, phantasmagoria, and self-deception, with its resultant suffering. The only answer is to clear the mirror.

Hazrat Inayat Khan reveals in these pages what the stages of this catharsis are for the pilgrim, and he shows how susceptible travellers on the path are to suggestions (particularly to danger of negative autosuggestion), which build up mental impurities.

When consciousness is refurbished, mind becomes crystal clear, and one begins to develop extraordinary powers of perception, acuity, intuition, even prophecy. One's dreams and visions become revealing. One sees the cause behind the cause and the purpose beyond the purpose of all situations instead of being obsessed by their outward appearance.

He who discovers meaningfulness attains purpose in his life. Only to the narrowed-down individual mind does the word impossible make sense; to the God-conscious, the only acceptable concept is all-possibility.

Spiritual Dimensions
of
Psychology

Part One

PSYCHOLOGY: THE SCIENCE OF MIND

CHAPTER 1

Psychology, Science, and Esotericism

On the day when science and psychology come to a certain understanding, knowledge will be complete. But when I use the word psychology, I do not mean it in the sense that is generally understood, for the psychology which is known as a new philosophy is in a primitive condition. What I mean by psychology is the point of view of the thinkers; the way the wise look at life; the manner of the thoughtful; the ideas of those who know life more fully. Psychology is the science of human nature, human tendencies, human inclinations, and human points of view. The more a man touches the depths of this science, the more it enlightens him, making life clearer to his vision. Psychology is that which bridges material science and esotericism.

I should mention first that the terms *matter* and *spirit* are for our convenience: as far as we perceive life as something tangible, we call it matter; and what is not tangible as a substance but is nonetheless perceivable we call spirit. The knowledge of this we call psychology; and esotericism is that knowledge which is gained not by perception nor by tangibility of substance, but by revelation. So we can divide the three different aspects of science into science, psychology, and esotericism. Science cannot be complete without psychology, nor can psychology be complete without esotericism. It is these three that make knowledge complete, and it is by these that one can hope to understand life more fully.

There is a vast field of knowledge in the realm of psychology. The knowledge of imagination and the same turning into thought; the knowledge of feeling and the same turning into emotion; the knowledge of passion and the same turning into expression; the knowledge of impulse and its outlet; the knowledge of impulse and its suppression; the knowledge of attraction and the knowledge of its contrary effect; the knowledge of sympathy and antipathy, their origin and source—all these belong to psychology. Psychology is the knowledge of tangible things, yet not of solid things that one can touch. Therefore it is more difficult to explain the laws of psychology in words than to explain the laws of material science.

Perception must be developed and insight into life obtained in order to understand psychology better. It is the understanding of cause and effect in everything, in every action, in every aspect of life. Psychology is a steppingstone towards esotericism because it is the psychological attitude which leads one to esoteric knowledge. If a person cannot see the truth of esotericism or mysticism, it is because he is backward in psychology. If he is not able to see the hidden law, he will not be able to see that hidden love which is called in the scriptures God. Esotericism therefore is quite a contrary process to the process by which science is learned, for science is learned by analysis, while esotericism is obtained by synthesis. If a person wanting to obtain esoteric knowledge breaks things into bits, he is analyzing them, and as long as he is analyzing them he will never come to the understanding of esotericism.

Psychology requires two things: analysis and synthesis. By understanding psychology better, becoming accustomed to synthesize as well as to analyze, one prepares oneself to synthesize only in order to understand esotericism more fully. Therefore acquiring esoteric knowledge is quite different from acquiring the knowledge of science. It is like going to the North for one thing and to the South for another. The ancients therefore made the knowledge of science, of psychology, and of esotericism one knowledge, and they called it alchemy. It was very convenient to explain it to the simpleton as the process of turning steel into gold. Many who sought gold in life went into the pursuit of alchemy; and some, who went to the end, instead of finding, became gold.

There is a story told in the East which explains this idea in an interesting way. A king was anxious to find someone who really knew alchemy. Many came, but upon examination it was found that they could not make gold. In the end someone told the king, "There is in a village a person living who is simple, most unassuming; but they say that he has the knowledge of alchemy." The king sent for him immediately, and when he was brought into the presence of the monarch, the king expressed his wish of learning alchemy and told him that he would be given whatever he asked for. "No," said the man, "I do not know any such thing as you ask." The king said, "Everyone told me that you are the person who knows." "No, King," he replied, "you have found the wrong person." "Look here," said the king, "I am going to sentence you to prison for your whole life." He answered, "Whatever you wish to do you may do. You have found the wrong person for what you want."

"Well," said the king, "I will give you six weeks to think about it, and meanwhile you will be in prison. At the end of the six weeks I am going to have you put to death."

He was put into prison, and every morning the king came to the prison and asked, "Now have you changed your mind? Can you teach me? Now death is approaching, take care. Give that knowledge to me." He said, "No, King, go to someone else, who has got what you want; I am not the person you are seeking."

And every night the king went to the prison as a porter and swept his floor and dusted his room. He took food to him, sympathized with him, and did everything he could do for him, as a servant would. He would ask, "Is your head aching? Can I do something for you? Are you tired? Can I make your bed for you to lie down in? Shall I fan you to sleep? It is hot, it is warm!" Everything that a person could do he did at that time.

And so days passed, and one day remained before the time appointed for this man to be beheaded. The king visited him in the morning and told him, "Now you see there is only one day remaining before your death. This is your last opportunity of saving your life." He said, "No, King, you are looking for someone else, not for me." But that night, when the porter came, putting his hand on his shoulder he said, "Poor man, poor porter, you are so sympathetic. I will whisper in your ears a word of alchemy, and that alchemy will change you from steel to gold." The porter said, "I do not know what you say, 'alchemy.' I only know how to serve you, and I am only sorry that tomorrow you will be beheaded. That is the one thing that tears my heart. I only wish that I could give my life to save yours. I would be most thankful." The alchemist said, "It is better for me to die than to give alchemy to the unworthy. The same thing which I give you just now in sympathy, in appreciation, in love, I do not give to the king who will tomorrow take my life. Why is it so? It is because you deserve it; the king does not." He whispered in his ear the secret word. Instead of making gold he became gold.

In the morning the king came to give him the last warning. He said, "Now here is your last chance. That moment has come when you must be beheaded. Now you must give in or go to the place where you are to be beheaded." He said, "No, no." The king said, "But you have already given it to me." He said, "To you? I did not give it to the king; I gave it to the porter."

This beautiful story gives us an insight into the idea of alchemy. That process through which the king went to become a porter is the process through which the knowledge of esotericism is to be gained. The other process, in which the king demanded, was not the right way of acquiring that knowledge, which never comes that way.

The difficulty with esoteric knowledge at the present time is only this, that a man trained in science is not yet capable of attaining to that knowledge unless he goes through the process of psychological knowledge. In order to enter the gates of mysticism, the first thing for man is to understand what feeling is, what service is, what sympathy is, what sincerity is. It is a great fault of learning today that the sentimental side is kept apart, which is the most important side. It is like wanting a person to come, not with his life but as a corpse; as if in order to educate a person the life should be taken out of him, and he should be turned from a living person into a dead one. Therefore we find the death of heroism, the death of idealism, the death of souls who have made impressions upon humanity which have lasted for thousands and thousands of years. What is to be revived in the present generation is the capacity of feeling. It is thinking which is developed today, but what is needed now is the battery which stands behind thought, and that is feeling. And after feeling comes seeing, that seeing which is referred to in the word *seer*.

CHAPTER 2

Mind and Body

What is mind? One part of humanity considers mind as
something inexplicable, and another part of humanity considers
mind as an action of the brain. If this is so, the mind exists as
long as the brain exists, and when the brain is destroyed the
mind is finished. If this were so, all a writer's work of three or
four months, many pages and books, and all an artist's work of
ten years, a studio full of pictures, would be in the brain. But
where in the little brain would there be room for all this? This is
a very limited conception of mind. The voice reaches through
the wireless for thousands of miles, but the mind is much finer
than the voice. It cannot be limited and restricted to the brain,
although the brain is the medium by which thoughts are made
clear.

The mind is thought of as something small. We say, "My
mind, in my mind," and that which is called my always seems
smaller than the material body, "my purse" or "my grip,"
something that can be carried about. The mind is really much
bigger than the material body. The shadow of the body is much
larger than is generally known; by the practices of mysticism you

may learn how very far it reaches. And the mind is much larger than the shadow. I may be sitting here and sending my thought to Paris. But then it may be asked, "If I am here and my thought is in Paris, am I separated from my mind? Can I go out and leave my mind in the house and come back and find it again?" No, the mind has wings that stretch from here, not only to Paris, but to New York or to Russia, to Japan, to the North Pole, to the South Pole, and much further still. If I send my thought to a friend in India, if I send it without letting anything interfere with it, he will feel it in his life and something good will happen to him on account of my positive thought.

There is no mind without body; that is to say, before the body was made the mind was only an *akasha*, an accommodation. The experience it has gained through the body as its vehicle has become its knowledge; and it is knowledge that makes mind. The akasha which becomes mind after the body has been born on earth has already gathered some indistinct knowledge from several minds it has met while coming to earth; perhaps from one mind more than from others. In that case it has gained characteristics chiefly from one individual who has passed on from the earth. Besides, through the parents this akasha has gained the knowledge or the mentality of their ancestry, their nation, their race, and of the grade of evolution of the whole of humanity at that particular time.

All that the senses can perceive is outward, but all that the mind can perceive is inward. This means that imagination rises from the mind and that the mind can perceive it. Feeling, memory, concentration, reason, all these are perceptions of the mind. One can call the mind more the being of man than the body; compared with the mind, the body is just like the coat a person wears.

CHAPTER 3

Mental Creation

So absorbed are people in this visible creation that they very seldom think of the value of that other creation which exists within themselves. Those things that tempt, that attract attention, that are of interest, all these are pursued by so many persons, who therefore become limited and unaware of that creation within, which goes on unconsciously.

Really speaking, every man is a world within himself. But how little man reflects about it! He is always conscious of being just like a drop in the ocean, whereas he does not know of the other state of being, in which he is the ocean and everything else a drop.

There is a passage in the Bible relating how God created the earth, and then created the heavens. What does this mean? Was heaven created after earth? The meaning is that this creation which is around us is first impressed upon the mind, and then the mind creates its own world, its own heaven. It is the creation of mind, a higher world yet within ourselves. And this world may be heaven or it may be the opposite. As Omar Khayyam writes, in his poetry, "Man's heaven is the vision of fulfilled desire, / And hell is the shadow of a soul on fire." Which shows that desire is the source of heaven and its fulfillment; at the same time it is mental fire and disappointment, worry, anxiety, or torture that is the shadow of the soul on fire.

Centuries ago, Zoroaster taught that there are three kinds of sin and three kinds of virtue: those in thought, in speech, and in action.

A person always takes virtue in action as virtue, and sin in action as sin, never thinking about virtue and sin in speech or thought also. Sometimes man's thought is stronger than his speech or action. It is the experience of every mystic and every person who has gone through the spiritual path that thought power is much greater than that of speech or action. In our everyday life we find that if we think of a person bringing a certain book or flower we desire, we often find he comes to see us, bringing that book or flower with him. We had not expressed the desire, and yet it has been done. Such is the power of thought, the creation of mind.

"Thoughts are things," as it has been said, but they are more. Thoughts are *beings*. They are as living as we; they work as we work. They have life in them. Christ said, "The words that I speak unto you, they are spirit and they are life." The spirit is the real life. Man is spirit. The body is matter. The body can generate, but cannot mind generate also? It is the generation of mind which we call thought or imagination. Thought is controlled; the other is not controlled.

There is a saying in Sanskrit, "There are numberless gods and yet there is one God." This means that as every planet is a world, every mind is a world; it is a living world.

The question is, if we make our world and mold our life, why should we have unhappiness, why troubles in life, why failures in life? The answer is that it is the fault neither of the Creator nor of the world. It is the fault of our ignorance, our lack of knowledge. Buddha pictures this lack of knowledge in this way:

it is as if you are clinging to the branch of a tree in the thick darkness of night, so that you cannot see what is beneath you, whether it is land or sea. Then you are always afraid of falling. You keep on clinging to the tree, and yet you are suffering with the fear of how long it will be before you have to let go. How long can you cling to the branch? Yet under your feet there is nothing! Such is life until light comes. Then it is like the coming of the sun. When the sun rises you find there is no water, for the land is just beneath your feet.

The land of immortality is so far from us, but when the sun of knowledge rises we see that it is near, so near! Once man knows that, he need not be taught morals or virtue: he knows what is best for him, whither to go; he knows his own creation. He knows that if he creates hideous spirits in his thoughts they will become monsters, and will work against him, and he will ruin his own life. But if man creates the spirit of love and kindness, others will help him in his want, and he is always surrounded by love and kindness.

Once people realize this, their life becomes different. They become the healers of men; they sympathize with the trouble of another; they serve in the difficulty of another; they seek to know if they cannot do something, cannot help in some way. A word may help, a thought of kindness and of sympathy will help. Whatever they do to others they do to themselves, because every thought of kindness or goodness and sympathy generates a world of sympathy around it, and such persons cannot be without it. If they go to a land where no one knows them or understands them, they can draw sympathy and love if they have created that within themselves.

That shows how important it is to be careful of what we say. A person acts under the spell of anger, says such things as, "I don't wish to see his face," any evil words—and he wishes he had not said or done such things after the spell has gone; not even to an enemy does he wish to have said these things. But at the time he did not know that what he created lives. That which he has created he will be afraid of, and it will become his enemy as well as the enemy of the person against whom his wrongful thought was directed. Not only that, but he will generate many more of the same kind. Once one bad thought is created in the spirit of anger or annoyance, there are a thousand other spirits created out of it. A world may be created by giving outlet to one single weakness!

All that we collect and gather in the external world for our happiness and comfort (as perhaps an estate) is limited; not even a thousandth part of this world that we possess can we call really our own kingdom, our world. But our mind can create and collect numberless thoughts and impressions which all make up its real world. All our possessions, all that we collect in life, all these things which we have to leave one day are momentary; but that which we have created from our thought, from our mind, that lives.

A person thinks, "Oh, someday I should like to build a factory." At this time he has no money, no knowledge, no capability, but a thought has come of someday building a factory. Then he thinks of something else. Perhaps years pass, but that thought has been working constantly through a thousand minds, and a thousand sources prepare for him that which he had once desired. If a person can look back in his life, at what he thought of at different times, he will find that the line of fate (which in the East we call *kismet*, destiny) is formed by our thought. Thoughts have prepared for us that happiness or unhappiness which we experience. The whole of mysticism is founded on this.

If thoughts can accomplish this, so can love or imagination. Even a dream can accomplish things, according to the impression which it makes. Some thoughts are as things, as objects; other thoughts are as beings. Some thoughts are as angels by our side and some are as devils. They are all around us, either helping us towards the accomplishment of the objects before us or drawing us back from those things we wish to accomplish.

One person thinks, and perhaps the result of his thought is very feeble; another has a thought today, and tomorrow the desire is fulfilled. Why is this? It is because of the power of thought. In the thought of one person there is more life; in that of another, less life. We call that life which has consciousness and activity; we call that an object which lacks intelligence and consciousness. Yet, really speaking, both are alive. The difference between an object and a living thing is that there is less life in the one than the other. A person with a weak will has no strength in his thought. If he thinks something a thousand times, it has no effect, because he has not that vitality or energy which is necessary for thought to live.

What is the vitality which gives life to the thought? It is the same as that in man, in the vegetable, in the mineral. In the one case the life is on the surface; in the other it is covered. That is why we use the word things in the one case and beings in the other. So there are dead thoughts and there are living thoughts. To which class a thought is to belong depends on will power: when there is will power, the word is both spoken and done.

This idea is expressed by the words *kalpa vraksha*, "the tree of desire." The story is that whoever should happen to come under this tree and sit down for a moment will have whatever wish he may desire fulfilled. Yet nobody knows where this tree is to be found. The tree is the mind; its root is the heart.

That which gives power to thought, gives spirit or life to thought, is feeling. A man without feeling is as dead; with feeling he is living, and so is his thought. Thought with feeling is a much greater power than thought without feeling. Merely to say, "I like your art so much," will have no effect when there is no feeling behind it. It is just a string of words; there is no life in it. But when those words are uttered with feeling, they go through your heart also, and the thought becomes living.

There have been great people whose loving thoughts would make anybody alive, who could impart life and could heal. They have left their thoughts behind them, and people have treasured them as scriptures, as holy books. They have taken them for a religion. Such thoughts can never vanish, such a long life has been given to them. Whatever form their thoughts have taken—music, prose, poetry, aphorisms, groups of words—they will never die; they will live forever.

CHAPTER 4

Divine Mind

The mind is that faculty, that intangible, imperceptible activity, of which the brain is merely a vehicle. Man limits things that are unlimited and beyond his power of measurement, and therefore he has pictured God in human form or given sacredness to the forms of animals. A person of larger mind has a larger view, and perhaps sees God in everybody; whereas one with a mind always desiring to find some evil will be able to find a spot of evil even in a good person. That is, from childhood onwards, man is accustomed to measure and understand things from his way of understanding, and to examine them in the limited way peculiar to himself.

"There is nothing new under the sun," said Solomon. People keep claiming to have found something new, but it may have been discovered and rediscovered a thousand times in days gone by.

The Vedas, which represent the ancient philosophy of the Hindus, in Sanskrit, the mother of languages, use the word *manu* or *manushi* for *man* and *manas* for *mind*. The English word *man* has the same origin. This shows that the origin of man's being is his mind; but his external form is so much before his eyes that it hides the other aspect of his being which in comparison to this seems invisible.

In Arabic it is written, "If you wish to know God, you must know yourself." How little man knows whilst he is in the intoxication of individualism! "I am a separate being; you are another; there is no connection between you and me, and we all have our own joys and free will." Did man but know how much his life is dependent not only on the objects and things that keep the body alive but also on the activity of a thousand minds in a day! Every time a man laughs it is the reflection of his mind, controlled by the power of another person's mind. Why does he feel sometimes sad, sometimes glad, sometimes cheerful, sometimes enthusiastic, sometimes tired without reason, sometimes depressed and exhausted? We meet so many minds throughout the day and night which are reflected on our own mind; and so the thoughts are changed, seemingly without reason. Yet the whole activity of life depends on these thoughts, and is changed according to them.

Who, then, can say, "I am an individual, independent and free. I can think what *I* wish, and I can do what *I* wish"? You are not doing what you wish; you are not thinking what you wish. There are various thoughts around you in the form of men and animals and individuals who influence your mind and feeling and thought; you cannot escape them. No one can escape being affected by another person's mind. There is always some person stronger than you, and always someone weaker than yourself. We are connected with one another. Our lives are tied together, and there is a link in which we can see one current running through all. There are so many globes and lamps, and yet one current is running through all.

The mystic seeks to realize this constantly and impress it on his mind in whatever he may see. What, for him, are the waves of the sea? Are they in the sea? They are individual only so far as one wave rises and falls. It rises and falls, but it merges into the sea. The new wave is a different wave altogether. What, for him, is the tree? There is one stem. The leaves spring from it, change their color, and drop off, but at the same time the life of the whole tree depends on the root and stem, and any damage done to either of these affects every branch and bough, every part of the tree. What, for him, is the body? Eyes, nose, head—which of them is "self"? The hand has a separate name; the fingers have a separate name; every part has a different name. Myriads of thoughts, myriads of imaginations, myriads of feelings—can we ever number their variety? The different emotions, the different ways of sorrow, the different grades of joy—can we ever distinguish them or classify them? Our being has so many aspects, and what is it after all that calls itself "I, me"? It is one, not many. It is only that if we had no body or mind, we could not realize that we exist. Through all this variety one realizes that, "I am one." The same things work further in mind till one finds that oneness which exists behind all these numerous names and forms, and in which one will unite with the Lord.

This shows that the experience of individuals, that is the thoughts, feelings, and knowledge of individuals, and the experience of the multitude of nations, of races, throughout all ages and periods of history has not only belonged to individuals, to the multitude, to the nations, the races, but has always gone back till it returned to that depth where it assimilated with what is called divine mind.

All minds are the different leaves of one tree. Some minds are branches and some are boughs of the tree, but there is just the one source to which all are attached. Not one object or life can exist that has not one central point in which everything meets and joins together. And that meeting ground is the divine mind.

The Brahmans therefore taught people to bathe at the point

where all rivers meet; the purgation of life was by bathing at Sungam. Those who really understood it knew that this pictured the divine mind. The purification in life lies in reaching that depth of life's sea at which the myriads of forms and names all join. The activity of all beings is directed from that center. As the Qu'ran says, "No single atom moves independently of the hand of God." That is, no activity of any kind takes place, either here or in the starry space, without the impulse from within and from that depth of life where all minds and the effects of all activity unite.

Coming now to the moral side of the subject, we ask, "In what way should we carry on our life? Should we be satisfied to depend on one power working?" No. That would be just like paralysis of a part of the body. The hand would not get up. Just think, where have your thoughts and impulses come from?

We may ask, "Should we then realize every impulse that comes? Should we not take action in every case, seeing that all come from God?" No, for it is the realization of mind that makes things right or wrong, good or bad, spiritual or material. It is your own thought, not the action. It is as you make it. Although the impulse is from within, if it is wrong you have made it wrong; if it is right it is because you make it so. The law justifies you. There is no other law. It is your law.

Whether a mind is stupid or wise, wicked or virtuous, every mind loves good and beauty. What is good? Good is that which is beautiful, which you admire, which you cannot help admiring. You admire the beauty of a person's kindness, the beauty of action, feeling, and thought. Nobody tries to see ugliness or to follow the path of evil. Is there anyone who will say, "Please do not be kind to me; please deceive me"? No one likes to be fooled. Wickedness is to seek to gain and not to give; but the wicked person is still awake to beauty.

The mystic is guided by his own mind. That which we seek in life we must give to another: if kindness, give it; if goodness, give it; if service, give it. The whole secret of happiness in life lies in this. When we seek happiness in the kindness of another, it means that we depend on him to make us happy, and as long as we look to another to make us happy we keep expecting that which we ought ourselves to have given. Not until we realize this do we know what justice is.

The world is a dome, where every action is the echo of another. Do good: it will come back; if not from one person, it will come from another. That is the echo. You do not know from which side it will come, but it will come a hundredfold more than you give.

Give love: will you get coldness? Do good: can you get evil? If you do good, do not judge your action or the action of another. You cannot be a judge until you are yourself selfless. Only then will justice come to you, only then will you understand the nature of justice. Self is the wall between you and justice. There is only one thing that is truly just, and that is to say, "I must not do this." When you say this to another person you may be wrong.

The mystic develops his mind in this manner, purifying it by pure thought, feeling, and action (pure meaning free from the sense of separateness), only following this one line of thought. Whatever differences in principles of right and wrong religious faiths may show, no two individuals will ever differ in this one natural principle: every soul seeks after beauty; and every virtue, righteousness, good action, is nothing but a glimpse of beauty.

Once he has this moral, the Sufi does not need to follow a particular belief or faith, to restrict himself to a particular path. He can follow the Hindu way, the Muslim way, the way of any church or faith, provided he treads this royal road: that the whole universe is but an immanence of beauty. You are born with the tendency to admire it in every form, and you may not blind yourself by being dependent on one particular line of beauty; you will not get it from another. You give it. You make yourself, your action, your thought beautiful, and let others get your beauty.

What is the perfection of mind that we have to touch? It is touched through contemplation, through realization, and through understanding of the one current running through the whole life. We begin to contemplate on that. The mind, which we call in religious language the Almighty and in mystical language the divine mind, is the depth of life, the depth of activity to which all activity and every activity is connected.

There is the whole religion. The mystic's prayer is to that beauty, and his work is to forget the self, to lose himself like a bubble in the water. The wave realizes, "I am the sea," and by falling into the sea prostrates itself to its God.

"Be ye perfect, as your Father in heaven is perfect."

Part Two:

THE NATURE OF THE MIND

CHAPTER 5

Thought and Imagination

Thinking can be divided into two parts: imagination, which is an outcome of the autonomic action of the mind; and thought, which is a result of its intentional action. A thoughtful man, therefore, is not necessarily imaginative, nor an imaginative man thoughtful. Both qualities have their place. A person who is accustomed to thinking and who is not capable of imagination is far removed from that beauty which is expressed in poetry and music, as these come from imagination. When the mind is given a free hand to do as it likes, it dances, as it were, and out of its gestures a picture is created, call it art, poetry, or music. In whatever form it expresses itself, it is beautiful.

Many people laugh at an imaginative person. They say, "He is in the clouds; he is dreaming." But all works of art and music and poetry come from imagination, for imagination is the free flow of the mind when the mind is allowed to work by itself and bring out the beauty and harmony it contains. But when it is restricted by a certain principle or rule, then it does not work freely. No doubt among artists and musicians you will find many who are dreamers and impractical people, but that does not mean they are less gifted. Perhaps their impracticality in some way helps them to accomplish something that practical people cannot. One need not follow their example, but one can appreciate it just the same. Besides, no one has believed in God, no one has loved God, and no one has reached the presence of God who has not been helped by his imagination. Those who argue with the believer and say, "But where is God? Can you show me? How can you conceive God? How do you explain God?" are the ones without imagination. No one can give his own imagination to them. Can anyone believe in the belief of another? If one can believe in anything one must do it oneself. And of what is that belief formed? Of imagination. It has been said, "If you have no God, make one," and no one has ever reached God who has not been able to make God. Those who trouble themselves about the abstract God have no God; they only use the word. They have the truth, but they do not have God.

Truth without God is not satisfying. One ought to reach truth through God; it is that which gives satisfaction. If all the strength that one derives from food were given in one pill, it would perhaps keep a person alive, but it would not give him the joy of eating. If one took the pill of truth, maybe a part of one's being would be satisfied, but that is no real satisfaction. The idea of God feeds a person; he must first make it in himself, with his imagination. But if he is not willing to use his imagination, if he is only waiting for God to come to him, he will have to wait a long time.

One might ask if it is good to have a strong imagination. It is good to be strong oneself. If one has strength, then imagination is strong and thought is also strong. Furthermore, a strong imagination means strength going from oneself, reaching out without one's control. Therefore a strong imagination is not always promising; it is strength of thought which is desirable.

For what is thought? Thought is self-directed and controlled imagination.

The difference between the thoughtful and the imaginative man is that the one thinks with will and the other without will. When once a person knows the value of will, he then recognizes that there is nothing in the world which is more precious than will. Naturally, therefore, the question arises in the mind of the thoughtful man, "Have I will in me? Have I a strong will or a weak will?" The answer is that no one can exist without will; everyone has a will.

The automatic working of the mind produces imagination, and the value of imagination depends upon the cultivation of the mind. If the mind is tuned to a higher pitch, then the imagination will naturally be at a higher pitch; but if the mind is not tuned to a high pitch, then the imagination will not be at that pitch.

Imagination has its place and its value. But when is it valuable? At that time when the heart is tuned to such a pitch that the imagination cannot go anywhere else but into paradise. The heart which is tuned by love, harmony, and beauty, without willing it begins to float automatically; and in this automatic movement it reacts to whatever it touches, or it expresses it in some form. When it is in the form of line or color or notes, then art, painting, music, or poetry is produced. It is then that imagination has value. But when it comes to business and science and all the things which are connected with our everyday life in the world, it is better to leave imagination aside and work with thought.

As both night and day are useful, as both rest and action are necessary, so both thinking and imagination have their place in our life. For instance, if a poet used his will to direct his imagination it would be a thought and would become rigid. The natural thing for a poet is to let his mind float into space, and whatever it happens to touch, to let his heart express it.

Then what is expressed is an inspiration. But when a person has to attend to a business affair he must not let his heart float in the air; he must think of the things of the earth, and think about figures very carefully.

When a person thinks, he becomes reasonable, exact, and thoughtful. Both an imaginative and a thinking person may go to extremes and may fail, but keeping the balance is what brings about desired results. A thinking person also may think so hard that he becomes confused by his own thoughts. There are many thinkers who think so hard that they become thoughtless.

Now going into the deeper metaphysics, what is it that forms the thought picture? This is a very subtle question. A materialistic scientist will say that there are thought atoms which group and make the form; joining together they compose the thought form. And if he wants to make it more objective, he will say that in the brain there are little thought pictures just like moving pictures, and that moving successively they complete a form. For this person does not see further than his body, and so he wants to find out the secret of the whole of life in his body and in the physical world.

In reality the brain is only an instrument to make thoughts more clear. Thought is greater, vaster, deeper, and higher than brain. The picture of thought is made by the impressions of mind. If the mind had had no impressions, the thought would not be clear. For instance, a blind person who has never in his life seen an elephant will not be able to form an idea of an elephant, because his mind has not the form ready to compose at the command of the will. For the mind must know a thing first in order to compose it. Therefore the mind is a storehouse of all the forms which a person has ever seen. But cannot a form be reflected upon a blind person's mind? Yes, but it will remain incomplete. If a thought is projected on a blind person, he takes only half of it; for he will not have that part which he should take from his own mind, and so he only takes the reflection which is projected upon him. Therefore he has a vague idea of the thing, but he cannot make it clear to himself, because his mind has not yet formed that idea.

The form of a thought which the mind holds is reflected upon the brain. The brain may be likened to a photographic plate. Both one's own thought and the thought of another fall upon the brain, just as reflection falls upon the photographic plate. But there is another process, and that is that the thought is developed like the photograph. And what is it developed with? Is there some solution in which the photographic plate is to be put? Yes, and it is the intelligence. Through one's own intelligence it is developed and made more clear to the inner senses. By inner senses is meant the inner part of the senses, for through five different outer organs we experience different things, and this gives us the idea of five senses, but in reality there is only one sense.

There are visionary people who have conceptions of the different colors of thoughts and imaginations and feelings, and different imaginary forms of thoughts and feelings. No doubt this is symbolical rather than actual. The color of a thought corresponds with the condition of the mind. It shows the element to which the thought belongs, whether to the fire element, to the water element, or to the earth element. This means that if it is, for instance, fire which is behind a thought, that fire produces its color around the thought as an atmosphere surrounding it. And when such visionary people see the thought form in the form of color, what surrounds the thought is according to the character of that thought.

A thought connected with earthly gain is of the earth element; a thought of love and affection represents the water element, spreading sympathy; a thought of revenge, destruction, hurt, and harm represents fire; a thought of enthusiasm, courage, hope, aspiration represents air; a thought of retirement, solitude, quiet, peace, represents ether. These are the predominant characteristics of thoughts in connection with the five elements.

There is no superiority of one element over another. The superiority of thought is according to the outlook of the mind. For instance, a person standing on the ground sees a horizon before him; this is one outlook. Another person is standing on the top of a tower and from there he is looking at the wide horizon; his outlook is different. It is according to the outlook that the thought is superior or inferior. Besides, no one can take any thought picture and say, ''This is an inferior thought,'' or, ''This is a superior thought.'' Thought is not an earthly coin which is inferior or superior: what makes it inferior or superior is the motive behind it.

Mind is the creator of thought and imagination. It is a soil upon which plants grow in the form of thoughts and imaginations. They live there, although as there is continual fresh growth, those plants and trees which have been created before are hidden from one's eyes, and only the new plants springing up are before one's consciousness. It is because of this that one does not think much about thoughts and imaginations which are past, nor are they before one; but at the same time, whenever one wishes to find a thought which one has once shaped, it is immediately to be found, for it still exists in the mind.

That part which consciousness does not see immediately is called subconsciousness. What is called consciousness remains on the surface, making clear to us that part of our thoughts and imaginations which we have just had and are still busy looking at. Nevertheless, once a person has had an imagination or a thought, it still exists.

In what form does it exist? In the form which the mind has given it. The soul takes a form in the physical world, a form which is borrowed from this world. So the thought takes a form which is borrowed from the world of the mind. A clear mind therefore can give a distinct life, a distinct form to the thought; a mind which is confused produces indistinct thoughts. And one can see the truth of this in dreams: the dreams of the clear-minded are clear and distinct; the dreams of those of unclear mind are confused. Besides, it is most interesting to see that the dreams of the artist, of the poet, of the musician, who live in beauty, who think of beauty, are beautiful; the dreams of those whose minds have doubt or fear or confusion are of the same character as their minds.

This gives proof that the mind gives a body to the thought; the mind supplies form to each thought, and with that form the thought is able to exist. The form of a thought is known not only to the person who thinks, but also to the one who reflects the thought, in whose heart it is reflected. Therefore there is a silent communication between people, the thought-forms of one person reflecting in the mind of another. And these thought-forms are more powerful and clearer than words. They are very often more impressive than a spoken word, because language is limited, while thought has a greater scope of expression.

CHAPTER 6

Suggestion

We hardly realize how much we depend in our everyday life upon suggestion, especially in forming our opinions of other people. Any praise or blame of a person that falls upon our ears soon appears to us as reality; and few there are in this world who reject a suggestion that comes to them from someone else, though they are quite ignorant of the facts themselves. We may become quite prejudiced against someone whom we have never seen, never known, merely because of what another person has said. And the most interesting part of it is that we are doubtful of praise, but credulous as to blame. The reason for this is that our experience makes us pessimistic. All the wickedness and evil that we meet with in life impresses us, and in time makes us feel that if anything exists it is wickedness, it is evil. When we hear good of anyone we begin to doubt it; we think that it is perhaps a mistake on the part of the person who tells us, that perhaps he is ignorant of the facts, or that we should wait till we know more about the man who is so good. But as to blame, we do not try to wait for the time when we can meet the person and get to know him and see where the blame lies: we believe it immediately.

When we consider the psychology of the crowd, we see how often great people who have really worked for their fellow men, in whatever capacity, fall into disfavor when once people begin to speak against them! At this time when our life in the world is very automatic and we all depend upon what the newspapers say, we collectively change our opinions of people, day after day. We neither know the cause of their being praised, nor do we know much about why they are blamed.

When people begin to realize what suggestion means, many react wrongly against it. For instance, they think that to say to oneself, "I am well," is suggestion, and they wonder whether it is not wrong. But they do not know that from morning till evening we are impressed by suggestions coming to us automatically in different forms. The importance does not lie in receiving suggestions or in rejecting them; it lies in understanding what will benefit us and what will be detrimental. For example, a suggestion is enough to make people believe a house is haunted, and that in itself is enough to make them feel afraid or ill.

Suggestions about difficulties we have to meet will produce difficulties. Suggestions made by people who say, "This person likes you," "That person dislikes you," all act so much upon a man that very often he becomes convinced of something before he even begins to try and find out the truth about it. Among a hundred people we will hardly find one who wishes to learn the truth before he accepts any suggestion; very often he does not even trouble about it. To believe in something as soon as another has said it and to form an opinion immediately is the easier way: it saves one from troubling anymore about it. That is why we readily accept a suggestion, and so our whole life is full of suggestions. It is hard on the person about whom we form an opinion just by hearing something against him. In any of the different capacities, whether he be our relation, our friend, our servant, or our superior, in any case it proves to be unjust. And it does not end there. When once a person has heard something against someone else and has formed an opinion about it, his opinion acts upon that person and makes him what the other thought him to be.

In this way many do not develop in themselves a sense of justice, a capacity for understanding rightly, because they are dependent upon what others say. And when a man is in a position where he has to do with many people and his opinion counts, where his opinion changes the condition of people's lives, when that man lightly forms an opinion only from hearing about someone, many people under him suffer. This often happens with people in high positions. When they have neither time nor inclination to take the trouble to find out about others who are dependent on them or who work under them, and when they change their opinion just because another person has said something, it becomes very difficult. Often most devoted and faithful friends have broken their friendship because of this weakness of accepting a suggestion from another. Between relations and friends it happens frequently that there comes a break without reason.

The best way to react against a suggestion is to try and find out the facts. But very often what a person does is to try and find them in the light of that suggestion. It is just like the story of Othello, who when he begins to enquire about Desdemona interprets everything in the light in which it was suggested to him.

According to metaphysics, one way of removing the effect of suggestion from the mind is by concentration. There are two things one can accomplish by concentration: one is to establish a thought in one's mind, and the other is to remove it. When one practices concentration, one is able to remove any thought one wishes, and to implant a thought which one wishes to keep in one's mind.

But besides this, from a moral point of view one should close one's ears and eyes to all that is disagreeable, inharmonious, and ugly, to all that sets one against another. One should not take notice of it. There is much beauty to be observed in our lives, if we can only turn our eyes away from all ugliness, from all that is undesirable, and fix our eyes on all that is beautiful and agreeable. For if we want to feel hurt and insulted and troubled, there is not one thing only, there are a thousand things that trouble us. The only way of getting over them is not to notice them.

Some people always seem to prefer the opposite to a given suggestion. That is another weakness. It shows that not only do they not trust another person, but they do not trust themselves either. The natural or normal state of mind is to have mastery over things, over conditions, and if a suggestion comes from another person, to think about it. By thinking about it we do not need to believe it, but we need not act against it. For all things are suggestions, whether they be good or bad. It is not that suggestions are always wrong: suggestions are often very good, but when a person is always against any suggestion, he will reject all that is good because he is afraid.

There are many people in this world who will defend themselves before they are attacked. No one has any intention of attacking them, but they are already on the defensive. There are people who before anyone has insulted them are on the warpath: even before anyone insults them they imagine that someone had that intention. These are wrong tendencies of the mind, and they should be fought in order to keep the mind clear. To clear the path of life, the mentality must be kept clear.

To keep a harmful suggestion out of one's mind means a struggle, but if a person does not know how to struggle correctly he will continue the same suggestion by this very struggle. For instance if a person who is struggling against his illness says to himself, "I am not ill. I am not ill," since both the words *not* and *ill* are there, he continues both. Or if a person who is in

poverty says, "I am not poor," the *poor* is there besides the *not*,
and his poverty will stay with him. While he is struggling
against it he keeps it all the time before his mind; although he
does not want it, yet it is there in his own consciousness, and he
cannot get rid of it. One should act wisely in regard to
suggestion.

The nature of the mind is such that the first suggestion makes
a deep impression, and the following suggestion can only make
little impression. Therefore, if once a person is impressed by a
wrong thing and has formed a wrong opinion, it is most
difficult to change it. Besides, there are people who sit upon
their opinions. They do not hold an opinion, the opinion holds
them; and once they have formed an opinion nothing can
change it, for it is a dead opinion, just like a rock. Where the
rock is placed, it lies: it is not a living being that walks and
moves.

Humanity suffers greatly by this weakness which persists in
the human race; and as there is a lack of psychological knowledge in the world it spreads more and more every day. In
ancient times humanity suffered because it had to depend upon
the opinion of one man, but now humanity suffers because it
has to depend upon the opinions of ever so many people,
working automatically all the time. During the last years, how
many personalities came out to shine before the world, how
many became popular for some time, and how many fell into
disfavor! The reason is that the crowd works automatically and
does not know reality. What it knows is what it is told. If
through the newspapers or in any other way an opinion is
formed, it becomes the opinion of the mob. And often it is not
right; seldom can it be true. For the betterment of humanity
people should be taught from childhood to understand what
the automatic working of mind is, and what a difference there is
between it and the working of mind with will.

Can one overcome everything by suggestion? It can be done,

but it cannot be said. There are many very great things that can be accomplished, but when one wants to speak about them, it is too difficult. Not only will others not believe it, but a man will not be able to believe it himself if he begins to speak about it. If they were left unsaid, greater things could be done than one's imagination can conceive.

IMPRESSION AND BELIEF

Colors and forms automatically suggest to us thoughts or feelings. The colors we wear and the colors that are around us have an effect upon us and produce an atmosphere. I once happened to go to a newly-formed club, and some members said to me, "There is surely some evil spirit in this house, for since we have had our club here, every time we have had a committee meeting there has been a quarrel!" I directed their attention to the walls of the room where they held their meetings, which were covered with red paper. I said, "It is this red wallpaper; it appeals to the fiery side of your nature, and if there is any inclination to fight it encourages you."

The ancient orders of sages and saints and contemplative people knew this, and with this thought in mind they chose the colors of their dress and of their surroundings. This idea is overlooked today, and people take any color which is the fashion of the season, not knowing what it suggests to themselves and to others. And so it is with the forms of things. If an object is well formed it suggests rhythm and harmony, and if it is crooked it suggests the opposite.*

In ancient times there were superstitions concerning good and bad omens. One of these was based on the principle that every

---

*For details on the meanings ascribed to colors and forms, see Hazrat Inayat Khan's *Nature Meditations*.

color suggests to a person who is going to do some work whether he will be successful or will fail; the impression he gets from that color stays with him to such an extent that it has an effect upon his work. There was also a superstition that if one met a crooked person when going to one's work one would have ill luck: not only a person, but anything crooked one sees at such a time naturally impresses one's spirit with crookedness. Not everyone knows about the facial features, but every person is affected by them. He receives an impression from them without knowing it, for their form suggests something which he may not be able to describe, although he can feel it. It is a language without words; it conveys something, though it is not always easy for anyone to interpret it even to himself.

Pain and discomfort often continue through the power of suggestion. As soon as one feels discomfort or pain, the mind repeats, "I have a pain, I am uncomfortable," and this suggestion adds to that pain, like fuel to a fire. Very often a person becomes tired before he has done any work because a previous experience of tiredness suggested it to him. There are many cases of people who are tired because of an impression in their mind which gives them the suggestion that they are tired. It is the same with weakness. Once a person is impressed with his weakness, his feebleness of body, this impression continues to act on him; it comes as an inner suggestion. And if some good friend tries to help him by saying, "You seem to be very low today," then this only aggravates it.

There is another most important side to suggestion, and that is an impression on one's conscience such as, "I have done wrong," "I have done something which was unjust," "I was not fair; it was beneath my dignity." No doubt this impression is produced by the good side of a person's being, but often it results in something bad. For what happens is that first comes the idea of having done wrong, and then in time that feeling is blunted and a person begins to bear it and think that it is all right. But as the impression of having done wrong remains and continues to act upon him, this makes him do worse and worse. Thus a man who has been in prison very often continues to go to prison, continues to commit the same crime. The reason is that he is impressed by that crime, and the spirit which opposes it has become blunted. He is now accustomed both to his crime and to the punishment; in other words, he has become master of the situation.

We see the same with children. If a child is impressed by something it has done which is good and we admire it and say, "It is very nice," or if the child of itself thinks, "What I have done is very good," this continues to work in the child, and in this way it will improve every day.

It is because they recognized the power of suggestion that the ancient people gave their children names whose meaning would suggest to them certain ideas. Naturally if a person hears his name called by others a hundred times a day, he has something suggested to him a hundred times. He may not realize it at the time, but the depths of his consciousness receive the suggestion and he develops that quality, for such is the nature of the soul.

This idea is very little known to the world, but the more it becomes known, the more people will understand its value. There is nothing in the world that can give a deeper suggestion to a person than his own name, for he is called by that name all the time. And one should be thankful to those who begin to understand this idea so that they can spread it among their friends. There is an automatic suggestion in the name. Every time we hear ourselves called, this produces the feeling of that name, not only in our own consciousness but also in the minds of those who call us. Automatically a feeling arises, and all this works for our benefit.

Many give names thoughtlessly, or give names without meaning, and this of course has no result. When a person has been given a name which means, for instance, something like torture, the life of that person may become torture in the end. Also, if the parents who give the child a name are not inspired, then an automatic working of the cosmic forces may suggest to them a particular name, and that name then builds the child's destiny.

It has been the custom of the great mystics to give people better names in order to produce better results. Sometimes a name given by a sage or a mystic in a moment of deep feeling, a name which comes out of his heart, changes the whole destiny of that person from the day that it is given. The poor become rich, the stupid wise, the insignificant great or famous. This is not only an idea, but a frequent experience. There have been many such instances when people have received a name as a blessing from a spiritual man and their whole life has been changed. We know so little about the power of the name, but the more one studies this question, the more one will realize that a person's name can have a very great influence upon his life.

Nothing gives a stronger suggestion than a deep impression of success or failure, of weakness or strength, of good or ill luck, of sorrow or joy; and it is the greatest pity when a person is deeply impressed by his unworthiness. When this impression continues, where does it lead him? It leads him to a complete unworthiness, and naturally he will have to bear with himself. In that way the side of his nature which should oppose it becomes blunted, and this results in hopelessness.

There are many different drawbacks of this kind, as when a person says, "When I am among people I become nervous, I become timid. When I am asked to speak or to do something, I cannot do it." All these things are suggestions. Napoleon never liked to say, "I cannot." When a man says, "I cannot," he has made a suggestion to himself, he has weakened his power of accomplishing what he could otherwise have accomplished. To admit to oneself, "I have no force, I have no power, I have no thought, I have no intelligence,'' only means working against oneself.

Often people who are disappointed with the world say, "My heart has grown cold," but it is actually they who suggest to themselves that their heart has become cold. Others may say, "I can no longer love." But we have come from love, we are love itself, we are made of love; how then can we no longer love? All these suggestions which are undesirable and foolish work against our life. Then there are people who imagine that nobody likes them, that everybody hates them, that everybody is jealous of them. Nobody may hate them or even dislike them, but naturally when such a thought develops in their own minds it reflects upon others and creates in them the tendency to hate and dislike.

We should always remember that man is not created by God as wood is carved by the carpenter, for the carpenter is different from the wood but man is created out of the self of God; therefore all that is in God is in man. All the different powers and qualities that we need in life are attainable if we do not deny their existence in ourselves. But when we deny that they exist in us, then naturally life will deprive us of that gift which is our own. How can a man be fortunate when he believes and thinks that everything that he touches goes wrong? How can a man be loved when he carries in his heart the thought that everyone who sees him dislikes him, hates him, avoids him, works against him? Nobody is his enemy except he himself; by such an attitude one becomes one's own worst enemy.

This psychological idea should not of course keep us from cultivating the principle of modesty. If a man without learning says, "I am learned," it does not mean that he will become learned. If without having a voice he claims to be a tenor, this will not make him a tenor. If he has not got those qualities he should not profess them, though he may anticipate them and expect them. He should not say that he is not entitled to them;

he should say, "I am entitled to all that opens the door to progress." But as soon as a man admits to himself that he has not got that quality, that intelligence, that power, that gift in him, he himself drives his spirit out of that world.

The following story is an example of modesty together with suggestion. A slave named Ayaz was so highly favored by the sultan that the sultan made him his treasurer. The most precious jewels and gems were given into his charge. And those around the sultan felt angry about it, to think that a slave was raised to their rank and that he was given such a trust. They were always trying to point out faults in the slave to the sultan. One day a courtier said, "Ayaz goes every day to the treasure house, even when there is no need to, and he sometimes remains there for hours. He certainly steals precious jewels from the treasury."

Every day the sultan was hearing something against Ayaz, and at last he said, "If this is really so, I will go and see it with my own eyes." He went and had a hole made in the wall so that he could see and hear what his slave did there. The sultan was standing outside, looking into the room, when Ayaz entered and closed the door. First he opened the chest in which the precious jewels of the sultan were kept; then out of the same chest he took something which he kept there. He kissed it and pressed it to his eyes, and then he opened the package. And what was it? It was the same garment which he had worn when he was sold as a slave. He took off his courtier's clothes and put on that garment, and he stood before the mirror and said, "Ayaz, do you remember today what you were before? Nothing; a slave brought before the king to be sold. The king appreciated something in you. Perhaps you do not deserve it, but try your best to be faithful to the king who has made you what you are. Never forget the day when you wore this garment, that you may not raise your head in pride above those who work under you; and never allow your feeling of gratitude to leave you, for prosperity is always intoxicating. Keep yourself sober and thank God. Pray God to grant the sultan a long life, and be grateful for all that has been given to you.''

Then he took off his garment, put it back in the chest, closed the doors, and came out. The sultan approached him with open arms and said, ''Ayaz, you were the treasurer of my jewels, but now you are the treasurer of my heart. You have taught me a lesson of how I must stand before my King, before whom I was nothing and am nothing.''

This must be the attitude. He did not give himself a suggestion of his misery as a slave, but of the realization that he had come from that state to his exalted position and that he should prove worthy of it. When we become conscious of our unworthiness, of our limitations, it certainly helps us; yet it can only really help us when we hope to become better. But if we stop there, then we might just as well stay there forever. When a person says that he is too weak to become any better, he stays where he is; but when he admits to himself, ''Yes, today I am weak, but tomorrow I will be better, I will try to be better,'' that is the right attitude. We should never allow that spirit of mastery which is in us to become blunted by a feeling of inability, for the essence of life is hope, and when we hope for the better, we shall be better; it cannot be otherwise. Hopelessness is worse than death. It is better to die than to lose hope.

We are able to do anything if we choose to make the effort. The difficulty is that often we do not choose to do so. And why not? Because we do not believe: what is generally lacking in man is belief. Another interesting thing is this: suppose there were ten people sitting in meditation and Providence granted them a boon, to ask for as much wealth as they would wish. Would all ten ask for the same amount? No, because no two would agree as to how much could be obtained. One would ask for a hundred, another for a thousand, a third would ask for a million and a fourth for nothing because he would not believe that anything could be obtained.

Although the river is flowing with clear water, the different people who go to it will not all be able to take the same quantity of water. The one who has a glass will take a glass, another who has a pitcher will take a pitcher, a third who has a rubber bag will fill that, and the one who has brought a tank will take a tankful. And so it is with all of us in our lives: what we obtain is what our belief allows us to obtain, whether of wealth or virtue, power or rank or spirituality. What our belief does not allow us to attain to we do not attain to; we cannot attain it. It is difficult to say to what extent our belief allows us to attain, for we live in this world of limitation and we cannot believe beyond what we can see. What keeps us from believing is that we are impressed by the limitations around us, and we can never think of or believe in anything different from what we see.

How can one get belief? This is the most difficult question anyone can ask, for it cannot be learned, it cannot be taught; it is a grace of God. Belief is essentially the same thing as faith, but only when belief has become a conviction does it turn into faith. I remember my *murshid* (spiritual teacher) giving me, in blessing me, this wish: "May your faith be strengthened." Being a young man, I thought, "Is that all he is saying to me, not, 'May you be inspired,' or 'illuminated,' or 'prosperous,' or something else?" But when I think of it now, I know that in that blessing there was all. When belief is strengthened, then there is everything: what we lack in life is mostly due to our lack of belief. But again, this is not something that one can learn or teach or that one can give to anybody; it comes from the grace of God.

To affirm a belief is one thing, and really to believe is another. Many will say that they believe, but few really believe. Yes, there are moments when a person is under the spell of belief, but then there come other moments when he is under a spell of disbelief. If this condition vanishes and there comes a steady flow of belief, then, as a river reaches the sea, that soul reaches perfection.

WORD AND VOICE

It is in accordance with every impression which is made on us that our life works, and the greatest impression is made by the word. The Bible says, "In the beginning was the word . . . and the word was God." This tells us of the creative power of the word: the word is as creative as God Himself. In the East, in good families, children were taught when quite young to avoid words which might cause ill luck: such expressions as boys use, "I will kill you," "I will shoot you"; or as are used by girls, "I wish I were dead," "I wish that it was all destroyed." Children were taught never to use words with a destructive meaning, for as far as we know at a certain time a universe may be connected with the word of man, and the word he speaks may come true. If he has spoken of something he did not wish to happen, it would have been better not to have said it. People do not think about this. They say things as a joke that might cause serious trouble in their lives or in the lives of their friends, not realizing how great is the power of words in our lives. Therefore the great teachers have made a science of words, so that by the repetition of certain words a definite result can be produced in one's character, in one's circumstances. A person can even help another by the use of a certain word.

Man's character can be entirely changed by the repetition of certain words: the results brought about by their repetition are wonderful. Thus suggestion often proves to be the secret of a miracle. This is a field which still remains unexplored by science, and the more man gets to know about it—perhaps five centuries from now—the more he will begin to believe that behind suggestion the spirit of God is hidden, the secret of the whole of creation.

The tone of a spoken word, the music of a phrase, often suggest a meaning which is quite different from what these words and phrases really mean. Simple words such as yes and no convey different meanings with different tones; the music of a phrase may convey either a sincere thought or a sarcasm. Not everyone can explain very well what tone it is that makes the meaning different, or what music it is that changes the sense of a phrase; but automatically one may say an ordinary word or a phrase in a tone which one normally uses to express deep feeling. When this happens many plead that it is not their fault if they have been misunderstood, and that they cannot be blamed for having only said a few simple words—and indeed, if the same words had been said in another tone they would have been simple.

When we go deeper into this subject, we find that every vowel is suggestive of a certain feeling, and that therefore names and words have a certain effect upon the speaker and the listener apart from their meaning. For instance it is interesting to gather from the sound of the word why the flower should have been called *flower* and why the stone should have been called *stone*. We feel from the sound of *stone* that it is hard, solid; and we feel from the word *flower* that it is soft and beautiful. Those who speak without any knowledge of tone and music, those who have no intuition of how to express their thoughts and feelings in a proper tone, lose a great deal in life; for it takes away much of the sense which they wish to express in their speech, and often it even suggests something quite different from what they had meant. We very often hear people say, "I told him over and over again, but he would not listen," but this may be because they were ignorant of the tone and music of speech. There is a psychological reason why he would not listen: perhaps the tone was not right, or the music may not have been correct.

Voice has great mystery. The voice of the individual is suggestive of something, not only of his thought, feeling, and action, but of his grade of evolution, of his past, present, and future. If ten people say the same thing, we will find each of them suggesting a different sense, a sense which goes further than the words themselves. While the word reaches as far as the ears, feeling reaches further into the heart. It is the voice that carries a sense, a feeling, and it expresses so much that the more one studies it the more one finds that voice has a very great significance. When a person says, ''I spoke, but nobody heard me,'' he does not usually know that it was because of his voice that he was not heard. It was not what he said, but what his voice conveyed. Not everyone will notice it, but everyone will feel it automatically. Kind, wise, foolish, weak, or powerful personalities will all show their character in their voice. It would not be an exaggeration to say that sometimes a person's voice expresses quite a different meaning from what he says in words.

When we trace the secret of language in history, we find that many languages known to us today have come from just a very few ancient languages. But if we go further than history takes us, we shall find that all languages have come from one language, a language that the human race knew in its cradle, a language that man learned by intuition. The names he gave to everything were derived from what each thing suggested; he called things according to what he intuitively felt on seeing and feeling them. That is why the nearer we get to the ancient languages, the more we find the secret of psychological suggestion. For every word of the ancient languages has a psychological value and is suggestive of its sense in such a profound way that it is as if the word had come as a reaction to what the actual thing had suggested. Our minds, corrupted by the new languages which have themselves been corrupted by mixture, cannot conceive or fully appreciate that feeling which one finds in an ancient language, and which is suggestive not only of the meaning of the word, but of the nature and character and mystery of what it is identified with.

It is on this principle that *mantra yoga* was founded. Words which sprang from the intuition of the yogis and thinkers, words which conveyed meaning in a most profound manner, such words were collected for the use of the adepts, who repeated them and profited by this repetition. Mantra yoga means the science of words, words which were sacred and helpful in one's spiritual evolution. The yogis have worked on this principle for many thousands of years, and have discovered a great mystery in the power of words. Sufis of all ages have followed this principle of making use of words which are suggestive of a certain sense, a sense which one wishes to bring out and make a reality in one's life. No doubt it is necessary to know the meaning of the sacred words one repeats; this gives a thousandfold greater effect. And the spoken word has a greater power than silent concentration, provided there is power of concentration and sincere feeling at the back of that word.

The suggestion of sacred words first impresses one's own spirit, helping one to develop that quality, that virtue, that merit, that power of inspiration which the words suggest. And the mechanism of one's inner being is such that every word that one repeats so many times becomes each time more living, and then this mechanism goes on repeating the same word automatically. Thus if a person has repeated a sacred word for fifteen minutes, throughout the day and night this word goes on, as the spirit repeats it continually.

Another effect of this repetition is that the word is reflected upon the universal spirit, and the universal mechanism then begins to repeat it automatically. In other words, what man repeats, God then begins to repeat, until it is materialized and has become a reality on all planes of existence.

There are also dangerous words. There are actually so many dangerous words that one cannot warn people against them. In order to avoid words of bad effect there is a very amusing custom in India among certain people. Instead of saying, "When you were ill I came to see you," they will say, "When your enemies were ill I came to see you."

The mystics of all ages have attached great importance to the mystery of the word, and every adept who has persevered in the path of mantra yoga has always arrived at the desired issue. No doubt perseverance, patience, and faith, all three, are required in accomplishing a mystical work by the power of repetition.

MOVEMENT

Every movement has a greater significance than one can imagine. The ancient people, recognizing this fact, knew the psychology of movement, and it is a great pity that the science of movement and of its psychological effect seems to be so little known today. Movement is life; its absence is like death. All that gives proof of life in whatever form is movement; all that shows the sign of death in whatever form is the absence of movement.

Movements can be considered from different points of view, and there are several kinds of movements. There is a natural spontaneous movement, which is mostly seen by noticing the movements of an innocent child who has not learned them from anywhere, who is not influenced by having seen someone else making these movements, but just makes them naturally, expressing feelings which words can never express. When feelings of astonishment, of fear, of joy, of fancy, of affection, or of appreciation are expressed naturally, they reveal much more than words can ever say.

Then there are the movements which can be regarded as a language of people belonging to a certain community, a certain family, a certain country, or a certain race. The members of that particular community alone know that language; others are quite ignorant of it. These movements which have become expressions of language are not understood by the people of another country, but they are not the natural and spontaneous movements mentioned above which are like a language for all. For instance the eastern way of beckoning a person is with all one's fingers; it suggests, "I call you from my whole heart," and when a person calls somebody with only one finger it is not considered right. In Italy and other Mediterranean countries there is the same way of beckoning someone. In all the countries of the East the movements may differ, and there may also be some movements which are like those of southern Europeans; there are psychological reasons why these movements should be alike.

There is a great effect made on life by the suggestions that one's actions and movements make to oneself and to another. There are several actions and movements that act either favorably or unfavorably for us or for others.

The salutation that the Hindus make to each other means that we evolve by unity. Joining the two palms suggests unity; raising them up means evolution. The salutation that Muslims make, raising the hands upwards, suggests rise, in whatever aspect it may be. And whether one understands its meaning or not and makes the salutation with that thought or not, it has its effect just the same, to a greater or lesser degree. Many empires and kings have been brought down from their great glory by the method of salutation introduced in their court by their bitter surroundings. Those salutations were lowering the hands from above.

Habits such as crossing the legs while sleeping suggest a crossing, a cross against the walk of life, which means hindrance to all progress. People grind their teeth in the night, which naturally suggests destruction, and it has its effect in the way of destruction in life. People have the habit of clasping their hands upon their heads, which practically suggests the prevention of every kind of rise. They have the habit of folding their arms, which obviously suggests renunciation. When a Moghul emperor of Delhi went to see a dervish living in the woods, he and his minister saw the dervish sitting with his arms folded and his legs stretched out. The dervish saw them come and sit by him, but he did not change his position. The minister, wondering about it, made a sarcastic remark, "How long, O dervish, have you stretched out your legs?" He answered, "Only since my arms have been folded." Stretching out the hands suggests greed or want, and folding its absence.

Sometimes a person crosses our way before us when we are walking. Especially when we are starting on a certain essential work, this suggests hindrance. Sometimes the pen drops from our hand when we are starting to write. That means that what we are going to write will not have an effect. A glass might break before we drink wine, meaning life is not ready to permit us the happiness we want. If a bunch of flowers is brought to us when we are starting on a journey, it will suggest every kind of success. This shows that every movement around us suggests to us something and has its effect on our life.

The ancients in the East, in Egypt and in India, had mystical dances. Every dance had a whole story, and every story had its effect upon the one who saw it. It is said that the dance of Mahadeva conquered the heavens; the dance of Krishna made him victorious over Kounsa, the monster. So among the Sufis the dances of the dervishes have their meaning. Those ignorant of the psychological effect are always ruined if they indulge in the grace of movement. Vajad Ali Shah, the padishah of Lucknow, and the king of Burma were the victims of their dissipation in the beauty of movements. Magicians do all their work with objects that suggest, together with movements.

There are also individual movements, the movements an individual makes, showing thereby his particular state of health and mental condition; for one can read a person's condition by the movements he makes. And if one has insight into movements one can perceive by a person's movements whether his eyes and ears are in good order, or whether he has anything wrong with any part of his body. Movements also show the characteristics of a person, his attitude, his point of view, his outlook on life. The fineness or crudeness of a person's character can be traced in his movements, and his deep characteristics such as pride and humility can also be discovered from a person's natural movements.

Is it right to make movements? All is right, movements or no movements, because everything has its uses, everything has its meaning. It is the right use of all things that is right, and the wrong use of everything that is wrong. No doubt there is also a meaning in controlling the movements. If a person is allowed to go on with his movements we do not know where it will end, but at the same time by repressing movements one can turn into a rock; and so there are many people who, with beautiful feelings and fine thoughts, turn into rocks because they control their movements too much. Every day a greater stiffness comes over them, and this works against their original character. They may not be stiff by nature, but they become stiff because they are taught to control their movements too much, even to the extent of turning into a stone. One sees this happen frequently. By repressing a movement a person may have buried a thought or a feeling inside him, but if it is an undesirable thought or feeling it is just as well that by these movements it should be thrown out instead of being kept inside him; it is better that it is extirpated than buried in the heart. No doubt there is another way of looking at it, and that is from the point of view of self-control; but this belongs to asceticism, which is another subject altogether.

Then there are the more refined movements which belong to art. This art, the art of movements, can be divided into three different classes. To the first belong the grace and fineness of movements executed with skill and subtlety, the harmony that they express, and the music that they have of their own. The next is the movements which convey the meaning of what one says more fully. When the art of speech and of song is separated from the art of movement, this certainly takes away a great beauty and charm, for speaking, reciting, and singing go together with movements. And the third class of movements is to illustrate the feeling that is in music, to express or to interpret music in the form of movements.

But the most essential aspect of movement is that movement not only suggests the meaning for which it is intended, but that, according to its nature and character, it can make an impression on the person who sees it or on the one who makes it, an effect which can automatically work to form a destiny in his life. In ancient times every movement the priest made during a service or ceremony had a psychological significance, and accordingly it made an impression on those who attended the services. Not only do we attach a meaning to a movement, but a movement very often has a meaning in itself, and that meaning has an effect. A person can even harm himself or others, not knowing the significance of the movement he makes.

How can we know which movements are good and which have a destructive effect? All we want to know we can know and will know; often we do not know things because we do not care to know them. The field of knowledge is so vast and yet so near that once we are interested in a subject it is not only we who go towards it, but the subject that comes to us. To begin to discover the significance of movements, their character, their nature, their mystery, we have only to watch. Our sense of right proportion, our sense of beauty and harmony, will begin to show us what suggests destruction and what suggests harmony, sympathy, love, beauty, or fineness. We have only to give our attention to it and it will all come. But to describe which movement is constructive and which is destructive would take volumes. It is perhaps as difficult and as subtle as making out which word is destructive and which constructive, and what hidden psychological significance each word has besides its common meaning.

Furthermore, our life as it is now, so busy and so occupied with material things, gives us little opportunity to look into the deeper significance of life. It keeps our mind occupied on the surface all day long, so that we have become ignorant of what is behind the veil of the life itself which we are living, of the movements around us, and of the movements we make. It is a kind of intoxication, and it keeps us floating on the surface, ignorant of the depths of life, for we have no time to think of these things. Nevertheless, these things have their meaning, their significance, and their effect just the same, whether we know them or not.

The blessings given by the sages, the good wishes and prayers of the masters, were always connected with movement. The movements made the prayer alive; they insured that the blessings were granted. No doubt if movement is without silent thought and deep feeling it is less than thought and feeling; it is almost nothing. But when a movement is made with a living and sincere thought and with deep feeling, it will make the thought and feeling a thousand times more effective.

SUGGESTION IN PRACTICE

Practical suggestion has four different aspects. The first is the suggestion that is made to oneself, which is called autosuggestion; the second is the suggestion that is made to another person; the third is the suggestion that is made to the lower creatures; and the fourth, which is little known to the scientific world but which has always been understood by the mystics, is the suggestion that is made to an object.

Autosuggestion is something by which one helps oneself to be encouraged or to be discouraged, to be well or to be ill, to go down or to rise, to be happy or to be unhappy. There are two kinds of autosuggestion: the kind that one intentionally, consciously makes to oneself and upon which the whole mystical training is based; and the suggestion that one makes to oneself automatically, knowing neither its nature nor its results. The latter kind of suggestion is made by everyone to himself without knowing whether it is to his advantage or to his disadvantage; by it many go downhill and very few uphill. There are many who without knowing it are in love with misfortune. They will say outwardly, "I hate it. I don't want it. I don't want to be ill. I don't want to be unfortunate," yet at the same time unconsciously they continually suggest the contrary to themselves by thinking, "I am so ill, I am so unfortunate, I am so stupid, I am so weak."

There are also two kinds of suggestion that one makes to others. One suggestion is that which one makes to help another to be cured of all illness or to help him to improve his life or his character. And the other is the suggestion one makes out of foolishness or out of ignorance of its effect. For instance, someone says in fun to a friend, "I will shoot you today." It is a joke, but he does not know what effect that joke can have upon his friend. One easily says by way of a joke, "You will go bankrupt if you go on spending like this," or, "Do you wish to die? You will surely have an accident.'' One simply says it, not realizing what effect it could have, sooner or later, upon the other. Sometimes in order to show friendship a person says, ''But how weak you look! You are very run-down. You can't be feeling well!'' These suggestions often make a person ill.

Then there is the suggestion that one makes to the lower creation. All pet animals, such as dogs, cats, and horses, receive suggestion readily and act upon it. This shows that it is not true, as many say, that the lower creatures have no mind. They not only have a mind but they have a heart too, and very often it is more apparent and more alive than in so-called human beings.

And the fourth kind of suggestion is the suggestion that one makes to an object. In this age of materialism this is not understood by most people, but from a mystical point of view it is very often as effective and wonderful as any other suggestion I have mentioned. In ancient times a hero, before going to war, used to take his sword in his hand and speak words of friendship to it from the bottom of his heart. He would say, ''I have taken you in my hand so that you will be my support, my protection, and my friend on the battlefield. All else I leave at home, but you I take along with me, my friend, my beloved sword.''

A musician in India, before playing on his vina, used to greet his instrument, saying, ''You are my life, you are my inspiration, you are the means of elevation for my soul; I greet you humbly. You will stand by me when I play.'' No one can know of its effect except the one who has spoken these words; he knows what life he has put into the object. That instrument which was an object has turned into a living being.

All manner of practices such as invoking sacred names and repeating spiritual chants in a new house are suggestion and affect even objects. However foolish it may look from the outside, still the fact remains that all things and beings represent life, the one life, although some are more open to suggestion and feeling and others seemingly less open. But even the latter are also open to suggestion; it is we who are not open to see them receive it. The man who knows this mystery knows a wonderful law of nature. As soon as a soul is awakened to this mystery life begins to reveal itself, and the soul begins to communicate with life.

CHAPTER 7

Reflection

MAN AND ANIMALS

The mind world in the term of the Sufi poets is called *aina khana*, which means the palace of mirrors. One knows very little of the phenomena that this palace of mirrors has in it. Not only among human beings but also in the lower creation one finds the phenomena of reflection.

One wonders how the small germs and worms, the little insects who live on other small lives, reach or attract their food. In fact, their minds become reflected upon the little lives which then become their food. It is true to a certain point that animals have no mind: they do not have what the scientist calls mind according to his terminology. But according to the mystic, the same intelligence which is in man is to be found in a lesser degree in the lower creatures. They have a mind, but not so clear; and therefore, comparatively, one might say it is like having no mind. But for the mystic, though it may not be so clear, yet it is a mirror too.

Friendship, hostility, the fights which take place among birds and animals, their becoming mates—all this takes place, not as thoughts or imagination, but as reflection from one mirror to the other. What does it show? It shows that the language of the lower creation is more natural than the language man has made, and man has gone far off from that natural, intuitive way of expression. You may ask any rider about the joy of riding, which he considers greater and better than any other form of sport or enjoyment. He may not be able to give the reason of it, but the reason is this phenomenon of reflection: when the reflection of his thought has fallen upon the mind of the horse, their two minds are focused to each other and the horse knows where the rider wishes to go. The more sympathy there is between the rider and the horse, the greater the joy one experiences in riding. After riding on horseback, instead of feeling tired one feels exalted; the joy is greater than the tiredness. And the greater communication there is between the minds of the horse and the rider, the greater the joy the rider derives from it, and so does the horse. The horse begins to feel sympathy with his rider in time.

There is a story of an Arab rider who fell on the battlefield. There was no one near to take care of his dead body, and his horse stood there three days without eating anything in the scorching sun, till people came and found the dead body. The horse was guarding its master's body against vultures. The story is also known of a dog that howled three days after the death of its mate, and died at the end of the third day. That is the reflection by which they communicate with one another.

Often one sees circus horses and other animals working wonderfully according to the instructions given to them. Is it their minds? Have they learned it? No, they have not learned it; it is not in their minds. At the instant when the man stands there with his whip, the reflection from his mind is mirrored upon their minds. If they were left alone they would not work, they would not think about it. The reason is that, as it is said in the Qur'an, "We have made man chief of creation." This means that all beings around man, large or small, are attracted to his magnetism; they all look up to him, for he is the representative of the divine, and they unconsciously know it and surrender to it. Elephants in Burma work in the forests, carrying logs of wood, but it is the thought of the man who trains them, mirrored upon them, that makes them do the work. When one studies it minutely one finds that it is not training, it is a reflection; that what the man thinks in his mind, the animals are doing. They so to speak become the hands and legs of their master. Two beings become one in thought, as in the Persian verse, "When two hearts become one, they make a way through mountains." There can be a relation established between man and an animal, but it is difficult to establish that oneness among human beings.

There is the story of Daniel, who entered the cave of the lions, and the lions were tamed instantly. Did he will them to be so? No. It was the calm and peace of the heart of Daniel reflected upon the lions that made them quiet like him. His own peace became their peace. One might ask, "After Daniel had left the lions' cave, did they remain the same?" It is open to doubt. This does not mean that some remainder was not left there, but that the predisposition of the lions wakened; no sooner was Daniel out of the cave than the lions woke to lionhood again.

Very often birds and animals give warning of a death in the family. One might think that they know from somewhere, or that they have a mind that thinks about it, but the condition is reflected upon them. The condition of the person who is dying, the thought of those who are around that person, the condition of the cosmos at that time, the whole environment, everything there is reflected on their mind. And they know, they begin to express their feeling, and they become a warning of the death.

If it is a pet animal who mirrors, do animals project their thought and feeling upon the human being? Does man reflect the feeling of an animal? Yes, sometimes human beings who are in sympathy with a pet animal feel its pain, without any other reason. The animal cannot describe its pain, but they feel to what degree it is suffering. The most curious thing is that on farms one sees shepherds, reflecting the feelings of the animals, make noises, sing, or dance in the same way as the animals would, and showing in many ways the traits of animals.

It is most interesting to watch how the phenomena of reflection between animals and man manifest to the view of one who sees it keenly; and it explains to us that language is an external means by which we communicate with one another. But the natural language is this reflection which is projected and reflected from one to another. This is the universal language, and once this language is understood one can communicate not only with human beings but even with the lower creation. It is not a tale when people say that the saints in ancient times used to speak with animals and birds; it is the truth. Only they did not speak with them in language such as we use in our everyday life; they spoke in that natural language in which all souls communicate with one another.

Furthermore, bullfights take place in Spain and elephant fights are known in India, though it is not often that elephants fight in the forest. It is the mind of the spectators who wish the elephants to fight that gives a stimulus to their fighting nature, and that desire reflected upon the animals makes them inclined to fight the instant they are free. The thousands of persons who watch these sports all expect them to fight, and the expectation of so many minds being reflected upon these poor animals gives them all the strength and desire for fighting.

There are snake charmers who are supposed to attract snakes from their holes. Yes, there is the music of the flute, but it is not always the music but the mind of the snake charmer reflected upon the snakes that attracts them out of their holes. The music becomes an excuse, a medium.

There are men who know a magic to drive certain flies from a house or a garden, and it has been experienced that in one day's time one was able to drive all the flies from a place. It is his mind reflecting upon their little insignificant minds. The ability to affect the minds of insects is an evidence of power, not a peculiarity. No doubt the human mind is incomparably greater in power and concentration, and naturally it projects its thought upon the objects it chooses. It is only the one who knows how to focus his mind who can do so. If a man drives away flies from a place, it does not mean that he has in his mind a fly element; only that he can focus his mind upon flies, which another man would not be able to do because a person does not generally give his thought to it. He does not imagine that such a thing could happen; and as he does not believe it, he cannot concentrate his mind. And even if he did reflect, just for an experiment, he would not succeed.

The will power is developed by focusing one's thought on a certain object of concentration; and therefore one can develop that particular thing better than any other by one's will power. For instance, those who play the brass instruments in a band naturally develop the power of blowing instruments, and they will be able to play the wood instruments, the clarinet or flute. But at the same time if they have once practiced the horn, they can play the horn better than the flute, because there is blowing in both, but they are accustomed to that particular thing. So with concentration. For instance, if a snake charmer with all his power of attracting snakes went near the bank and wanted to attract a purse, he could not very well do it. He can attract snakes, but he cannot attract a purse. But no doubt once the will power is developed in any direction, it will prove to be useful in all things one does.

There have been cases where horses have been able to give the answers to complicated mathematical problems to which those who put the questions to them did not know the answer. It is the reflection of the teacher's mind projected upon the mind of the horse, for the horse is not capable of doing mathematics, nor can it be. It is a kind of mediumistic process by which a mathematical idea is projected upon the mind of the horse. It is possible that even the person who does it does not know it; but his very effort to make the horse do mathematics has shown the success. The power of projection can be increased with the increase of will power. It can be developed by the development of will, of thought, of feeling. There is so much that we could learn in little things, which can reveal to us the greatest secret of life, if only our eyes were open and if we were eager to observe the phenomena.

COMMUNICATION AND OBSESSION

The phenomenon of reflection differs in its nature and character, especially by reason of the nature of different personalities. In the first place, the person whose thought becomes reflected in the heart of another may have a concrete form in his thought, he may be able to hold it as one design or picture. In that case the reflection falls in the heart of another man clearly. But if the mind is so weak that it cannot hold a thought properly, then the thought is moving and it cannot reflect the mind of another. If the mind of the person is not in good condition, then the picture there is not clear. If a person's mind is not clear, if it is upset, if it is too active, then that mind cannot convey the reflection fully. The mind is likened to a lake. If there is wind blowing and the water is disturbed, then the reflection will not be clear. And so it is with the mind. The mind which is still is capable of receiving reflection. The mind which is powerful, capable of making a thought a picture, of holding a thought, its thought can project beyond any boundaries that may be standing there to hinder it.

One may ask, "Does the heart reflect the mind or the mind the heart?" In the first place it must be known that the mind is the surface of the heart and the heart is the depth of the mind. Therefore mind and heart are one and the same thing. If you call it a mirror, then the mind is the surface of the mirror and the heart its depth; it is the same mirror. Mirror is a very good word, because it contains both, the mind and the heart. If the reflection comes from the surface of the heart, it touches the surface; if it comes from the depth of the heart, it reaches the depth. It is just like the voice of the insincere person: it comes from the surface and it reaches the ears. The voice of the sincere person comes from the depth and goes to the depth. What comes from the depths enters depths, and what comes from the surface remains on the surface.

Nothing can remove two minds that are focused to one another. No person with an affectionate heart, with tender feeling, will deny that two sympathetic souls communicate with one another. Distance is never a bar to this phenomenon. Have we not seen in the recent war the womenfolk of the soldiers, their mothers, their wives, their children, linked with their dear ones fighting at the front, feeling their conditions, and knowing when a soldier was wounded or dead? Many will say that it is the thought which reaches another. But at the same time even the thought vibrations in the profound depth become a design. One thought, one design, one particular picture becomes reflected, and by its being so mirrored upon him, the other person feels it in an instant. Reflection is not like a conversation. In a conversation every word unfolds the idea, and so the idea gradually becomes manifested; but in the reflection the whole idea is reflected in one instant, because the whole is there in the form of a picture, and it is mirrored in the mind which has received it.

It is this theory which opens before us the mystery that lies in the connection between the living and the dead. The idea of obsession may be thus explained, that a reflection of the thought of someone on the other side, held fast by a living creature on the earth, becomes an obsession. A young anarchist may assassinate someone; in the end you will find that there has not been such a great enmity between him and the person whom he killed; there is a mystery behind it. Some enemy of the person who was killed, on the other side, has reflected his thought in the passive mind of this young person, who through his enthusiasm and strength felt inclined to kill someone, not knowing the reason himself, and caused someone's death. Especially among anarchists one finds such cases. Owing to their extreme points of view, their hearts are in a condition to be receptive; they can receive a good reflection or a bad reflection and act accordingly.

Is it possible that a person living on the earth should be able to project his thought on those who are on the other side? Every religion has taught this lesson, but the intellectual evolution of our time has not grasped it fully. For instance, among Hindus there is a custom today to offer to the dead person all that he loved in the form of flowers and colors, in the form of natural environments, the river, the stream, the mountain, the tree. All this that their dear one loved, his survivors make of it an offering to him. Among some people there is a custom of making delicious dishes, of preparing burning incense, flowers, and perfume. And then after offering it to the dead, they partake of it, because if they partake of it—it may seem strange—yet it is their experience which is reflected, and therefore it is right for them to partake of it though it is an offering. It is through them that the dead receive it; they are the medium for the offering, and this is the only way that they can give it.

This teaches another idea, that those who mourn their dear

ones certainly continue to give those who have departed pain, because instead of having a better experience and reflecting it to them from this world, they gather pain and offer it to their dead. The wisest thing that one could do for those who have passed is to project the thought of joy and happiness, of love and beauty, of calm and peace. It is in this way that one can help the dead best.

One may ask, "Can one influence a soul that has passed beyond this world to such an extent that one can make him exert a special action on the mind of another person on earth?" This is a thing possible in theory, but why trouble that spirit? If you are able to influence the spirit, why not influence the person who is on earth?

At the present time, when materialism is increasingly prevalent, very few recognize cases of obsession. Very often those obsessed are sent to insane asylums, where they are given medicines or different treatments. The physicians think that there is something wrong with the brain of the person, with his mind, that something has gone wrong with his nerves. But in many cases that is not so; that is the outcome of the obsession. When once a person is obsessed, naturally he has lost his rhythm, his tone, and therefore he does not feel himself; he feels queer. A continual discomfort causes a disorder in his nervous system, thereby resulting in different diseases, but at the root of it is obsession.

Obsession can be caused not only by the dead, but also by a living person; only in the case of the former it is called obsession, in the case of the latter it is called impression. But what generally happens is this, that the souls who are attached to the earth are either earthbound or the inspirers or protectors of the earth. The love of the inspirers and protectors of the earth comes like a stream. No doubt it might come to individuals, but at the same time it is mostly for the multitude. Therefore it cannot be classed with what we call obsession; it can be called a blessing. But when the other souls who are earthbound reflect, it is for the reason of a want; and however great a reason or a want may be, it is imperfection because it is limited. Besides, the creation is a phenomenon in which every individual must have his freedom, to which he has the right. When he is deprived of that freedom by obsession, however much helped, that person remains in a limited condition. Furthermore, it is possible that obsession may become most interesting, and if the obsessed one is cured of his obsession he does not feel himself. He feels that some life that he has experienced for a long time is taken away from him.

In short, both communication between living beings and communication between the living and the souls who have passed from this earth are in reflection, a reflection which depends upon the power and clearness of mind.

REPETITION

A thought may be compared with a moving picture projected upon a curtain. It is not one picture but the several parts of the picture that, changing every moment, complete it. And so it is with the thought. It is not always that every person holds a picture in his mind. As a rule a person completes a picture by a gradual process. In other words, the thought picture is made in parts, and when the thought is completed the parts meet to form one picture.

It is according to this theory that the mystics have made *mantra shastra*, the science of the psychological phenomena of words, which the Sufis have called *wazifa*, because for a concentration of thought the holding of a thought in mind is not sufficient. In the first place, it is not possible for every person; only for certain persons is it possible to hold a thought as a picture. If there is any possibility of completing a thought, it is only by repetition. It is therefore that eastern art shows the same tendency. If a border around a wall is made of roses, it is a rose repeated twenty thousand times, that the picture of a complete rose may be made at the end of one glance cast over it. If there are many objects before one, no object can one hold in thought. Therefore, the best way that the mystics adopted of contemplating was to repeat a word suggestive of a certain thought, a word that caused the picture of a certain idea by its repetition. Yet the repetition cannot suffice the purpose. In order to engrave upon a stone a certain figure, a line drawn with pencil is not sufficient; one has to carve it. And so in order to make a real impression of an idea deeply engraved on the subconscious mind, an engraving is necessary. That is done by the repetition of a word suggestive of a certain idea. No repetition is wasted, for every repetition not only completes but deepens it, making thereby a clear impression upon the subconscious mind.

Apart from the mystical process, one sees persons in one's everyday life who have perhaps repeated in their minds the thought of pain, of hatred, of longing, of a disappointment, of admiration, of love, unconscious of the work it has done within themselves; and yet a deep impression of it has been produced in the depths of their heart, and that becomes projected upon every person they meet. One cannot help being drawn to a loving person; therefore one is unconsciously drawn to an affectionate person. One cannot cover one's eyes from the feelings of hatred that comes from someone; one cannot ignore the feeling of pain that comes forward from a person, for the pain is engraved in his heart. This is the phenomenon of reflection, reflection of one mind upon another. People may sit together, work together, live together for their whole life, and yet they may be closed to one another. It is the same reflection. If the heart of one person is closed, its influence is to close the heart of another. A person with closed heart will close the hearts of others everywhere he goes. Even the most loving person will helplessly feel the doors of the heart close, to his greatest regret, not knowing what has happened. It is an unconscious phenomenon.

Therefore pleasure and displeasure, affection and irritation, harmony and agitation, all are felt without a word spoken when two persons meet. It is our words which hide reality. If we do not see, it does not mean that we cannot see; it only means that our eyes are not always open, so we remain ignorant of the phenomenon of reflection. If this is true, there is nothing in this world which a person can hide. As the Qur'an says, "On the Day of Judgment your hands and feet will give evidence of your doings." But every moment of the day is a Judgment Day. We need not wait till Judgment Day to see this phenomenon. We see it, we experience it always, yet we do not pay sufficient attention to it. Whenever we have a kind feeling, good will towards someone, or irritation, agitation, an antagonistic, hostile inclination, we cannot keep it from another. And this is sufficient for us to know that innermost truth, that absolute truth of the whole universe, that the source is one, the goal is one, life is one, and the many are only its covers.

THE EXPANSION OF THE HEART

The phenomenon of reflection is such that every action and every thought is reflected in oneself, and there arises a production. Something is produced which forms a direction in one's life and which becomes a battery behind everything one does, a battery of power and of thought. There is a saying, "Man's real being speaks louder than what he says." This shows that in this phenomenon of reflection every person is exposed to all the mirrors, and there is nothing in the world that is hidden. What one does not say, one reflects, so therefore there is no secret.

The words used by Solomon, "Under the sun," are for night and day both. The real sun is the intelligence. In the light of that sun all mirrors, which are human hearts, reflect all that is exposed to them without any effort on the part of man. This is the reason why the desire of a person, if it is a real wish, becomes fulfilled sooner or later: it is reflected, and through that reflection it becomes living. The reflection gives it a life because it is not in a dead mirror; it is in a living mirror, which is a human heart. It is nothing to be surprised at if you have just thought of a friend and the friend happens to come to meet you while you are going to do something else. It is unexpected outwardly, but inwardly your reflection rising in the mind of your friend has arranged your meeting.

Someone asked a sage, "Shall we meet in the hereafter those around us here?" The sage answered, "Yes, we shall meet those whom we love and those whom we hate." The person was rather pleased with the first thing, but much displeased with the other. The sage further explained, "You think of two persons, the person whom you love most and the person whom you hate most; you cannot help thinking of them. Either one can be praying for the friend or cursing the enemy, but he will be thinking often of both. And the most wonderful thing is that those whom you love or you hate in life, you meet unexpectedly without any intention on your part to attract them." The person asked, "What shall we do?" The sage said, "The best thing is not to hate anyone, only to love. That is the only way out of it. As soon as you have forgiven those whom you hate, you have gotten rid of them. Then you have no reason to hate them; you just forget."

The great Hindustani poet Amir says, "My eyes, you have the light of the Perfect One, and you cannot see. It is not the lack of light in you; it is only because you keep covered." Man is seeking for a clear vision, continually wanting to see light, and yet he covers his very eyes, the sight which has divine light in him, by covering his heart. No one can teach anyone, nor can anyone acquire, that power of seeing clearly. Man is naturally a seer. When he does not see it is a surprise. The seers not only see an individual when the individual comes before them; if ten thousand persons are sitting before them, they are capable of seeing all as a multitude and each as an individual. The reason is that the larger a mirror becomes, the more reflections it accommodates in itself. Therefore in one person a multitude can be reflected at one and the same time: hearts, souls, minds, and all. No doubt it begins with seeing the reflection from one person, but as the heart expands, so it takes the reflection of the multitude.

In this lies the mystery of the spiritual hierarchy; it is only the expansion of heart. Do we not see in our everyday life one person who says, "Yes, I can love one person, whom I love; but then I cannot stand the others?" It is only the limitation of the heart. There is another person who says, "Yes, I can love my friends, those with whom I feel at home; I feel a contact. But then not strangers; I cannot love them; I am closed." And he really is closed before strangers. He may be a loving person, but in their presence his love is closed. And in proportion as the heart becomes more free of this limitation, naturally it becomes larger; because the length of the heart, as Asaf has said in his verse, is unimaginably great. Asaf says that if the heart of man were expanded, it would accommodate the whole universe, just like a drop in the ocean. The heart can be so large that it can hold the whole universe, all. And the heart that can hold all can see the reflection from all, because the whole process of evolution is getting larger. Getting larger means getting freer from limitations, and the outcome of this condition is that the vision becomes clearer.

How can the minds of the multitude be reflected in the heart? In the same way that the picture of a group is taken on a photographic plate. There may be a crowd, the photographic plate will take them all; if it cannot take them, then it is not large enough. The heart is as capable as a photographic plate of taking reflection; if it cannot take it, it is because it is limited, it is small. The whole life is an absolute intelligence, it is a mirror land in which all is reflected. When we think of this deeply, we find that even in the daylight we close our eyes and sleep.

What we must first accomplish in life is to clear the reflections from our own heart, reflections which hinder our path. For instance, a businessman went to a mystic and said, "Well, I cannot understand. There is some sort of bad luck with me. I always fail, and I cannot understand why I fail. I went to some spiritualists, I went to some clairvoyants, I went to some people who make one's horoscope. Some said one thing, some another thing; now I cannot make out what is right." The mystic told him, "The right and wrong is in yourself. Listen to yourself. Find out what is going on in your mind. Is it not the memory of the loss that you have had? It is a kind of continual voice going on in your heart. The astrologers will say it is something that is around you; the spiritualists will say that some ghost or spirit is behind it. The real thing—though there may be ghosts or there may not be—is that in your heart a voice is saying, 'You have failed, you have failed, you have failed.' Can you make this be quiet, be silent? As soon as you get rid of this reflection, all will be well with you." He said, "What must I do? How can I do it?" The mystic said, "Determination. Promise me that from now on you will never give a thought to your past failures. Past is past, the present is present. Proceed with hope and courage; all will be well."

You will always find that those who say, "Everything is going wrong with me," are hearing the voice aloud; it is their own failure that is talking with them. As soon as they have been able to make this voice silent, the failure is ended; a new page in the book of life is turned, and they can look forward to their life with a greater courage and a greater hope. That person is brave who in the face of a thousand failures would stand up and say, "Now I am not going to fail. The failure was only a preparation for my success." That is the right spirit.

How can one wipe out all the innumerable pictures which hinder one? The whole process of the Sufi method is this, to make the plate of the mind clear. This can be done by the practice of concentration. The horses in the forest will not come if you call them to come to you, nor will they walk as you wish them to walk, because they are untrained. So are one's thoughts and imaginations: they go about in the mind without harness, without rein. And when they are taken in hand, then one is just like the trainer in a circus who tells the horse to come, and the horse comes; then he tells the horse to go and the horse goes; he tells the horse to run, and the horse runs, to stop, and the horse stops. Working with thoughts, one is just like the circus man. This is the first lesson and the most important lesson to learn in the Sufi work; this is the foundation of the whole mysticism and the practice of philosophy: that you be able to move your thoughts about as you want to. When you wish to think of a rose, a lily must not come into your thought; when you think of a horse, an elephant must not appear before you; you must keep it away. This teaches you to create a thought and hold it, and to expel every thought that you do not wish to have. In this way you become the master of your thoughts: you train them, you control them, and then you use them for your benefit.

Does this not prove to us that this is a mirror land, a mirror land with a living phenomenon, living because the mirrors are living? It is not only projection and reflection that take place in the mirrors, but a phenomenon of creation: that all that is projected and reflected is created at the same time, materialized sooner or later. It is in this that the Sufi finds the secret of mastery: that besides all the ideas of fate and of worldly and heavenly influences, there is a creative power which works in man. In one person perhaps the creative faculty of his being is at work one degree, and ninety-nine degrees are the mechanical part of his being at work. In another person, who is more evolved, perhaps ninety-nine degrees of creative power are at work and one degree of the mechanical part of his being. It is the mechanical part of one's being which is subject to conditions and environments, and which is helpless; and it is the creative part of one's being which is creative, which produces phenomena; and in this aspect the divine essence is to be found.

CHAPTER 8
Reason

When we analyze reason it opens before us a vast field of thought. In the first place, every doer of good and every evildoer has a reason to support his action. When two persons quarrel, each says he is in the right because each has a reason. To a third person, perhaps the reason of one or the other may appear to be more reasonable; or perhaps he will say that both have no reason and that he has reason on his side. All disputes, arguments, and discussions seem to be based upon reason. Yet reason is something which, before one has analyzed it, is nothing but an illusion, and it keeps one continually in perplexity. The cause of all disharmony, all disagreement, is the perplexity which is caused by not understanding another's reason.

But one might think, what is reason? Where does it belong? Reason belongs to both earth and heaven: its depth is heavenly; it surface is earthly. And that which fills the gap in the form of reason, between earth and heaven, is that middle part of it which unites it. Therefore reason can be either most confusing or most enlightening. There is the depth of reason, the most perfect reasoning, which belongs to heaven; and there is another reasoning which belongs to the earth. If a person says to someone, "Why did you take another person's raincoat?" he may answer, "Because it was raining." He has a reason; another reason is needed to think, "Why, I must not take another person's raincoat. Although it was raining, yet it was not my raincoat." That is another reason altogether. Do you think that thieves and robbers or great assassins have no reason? Sometimes they have great reasons; but their reason is on the surface. Can a thief not say in order to justify his action, "What is it to that rich person if he lost so much money? Here am I, a poor man. I could make a better use of it. I have not robbed him of every penny; I have just taken as much as I wanted. It is useful, I can do some good with it."

Reason is the servant of mind. The mind feels like praising a person: the reason at once brings forth a thousand things in praise of him, in his favor. The mind has a desire to hate a person: at once reason brings perhaps twenty arguments in favor of hating him. So we see that a loving friend can find a thousand things that are good and beautiful in his friend; an adversary will find a thousand faults in the best person in the world, and he has reasons.

In French conversation they say, "*Vous avez raison*," but one can say that everyone has reason. It is not sometimes that one has a reason; everyone always has a reason, only it depends which reason it is. Is it the earthly reason, is it the heavenly reason, or is it the middle reason? It is natural that heavenly reason does not agree with earthly reason.

Now coming to the essence of things, where do we get reason, where do we learn it? We learn earthly reason from our earthly experiences. When we say, "This is right and that is wrong," it is only because we have learned from the earth to say so. To an innocent child who has just been born on the earth and who has not yet learned to know right and wrong, it is nothing; he has not yet acquired earthly reason. There is also a reason which is beyond earthly reason. The person who has taken someone's raincoat has a reason, because it was raining, but there is a reason beyond that, that it does not belong to him. He should rather have gotten wet through in the rain than taking the raincoat. That is another reason; that is reason behind reason.

Then there is the sense of reason which is heavenly reason. Not everyone understands this reason; it is this reason which the seers, sages, mystics, and prophets discover within themselves. It is upon this reason that religions are founded; in the soil of this reason the ideas of mysticism and philosophy spring as plants and bear fruits and flowers. When a pupil is expected to listen to the reason of his teacher instead of disputing it, it is in order to recognize the heavenly reason behind it and to learn that there comes a time in life when one's eyes are open to the essential reason. And what is that reason called? That reason is called *bodhisattva*. *Sattva* means essence, and *bodhi* or *buddh* means reason; from this word comes the title of Gautama Buddha.

How is one to arrive at that reason? By arriving at that rhythm which is called sattva. There are three rhythms, *tamas, rajas*, and *sattva*. A person whose rhythm of life is tamas knows earthly reason; he whose life is rajas knows beyond earthly reason, a reason which is hidden behind a reason; and the one who begins to see or live in the rhythm of sattva begins to see the cause of every reason, which is in the profound depths of the whole being. That is God's reason.

Reason is attached to impulse and to thought. The reason which is attached to thought is the middle part of reason; the reason which is attached to impulse is the lower part of reason. But the reason which is inspiring is heavenly reason. This reason unfolds divine light; it comes by awakening to the reason which one finds living in the heart of God.

There is a story that Moses was passing through a country with Khidr, who was his murshid when Moses was being prepared for prophethood. Moses was first given the lesson of discipline, to keep quiet under all circumstances. When they were walking through the beauty of nature, the teacher and pupil both were quiet. The teacher was exalted in seeing the beauty of nature; the pupil also felt it.

And so they arrived at the bank of a river, where Moses saw a little child drowning and the mother crying aloud, for she could not help. Then Moses could not keep his lips closed; he had to break his discipline and say, "Master, save him, the child is drowning!" The murshid said, "Quiet!" Moses could not keep quiet. He said again, "Master, Master, save him! The child is drowning!" Khidr said, "Quiet!" and Moses was quiet.

But the mind of Moses was restless; he did not know what to think. "Can the master be so thoughtless, so inconsiderate, so cruel, or is the master powerless?" he asked himself. He could not understand which was which; he did not dare to think such a thought, and yet it made him very uncomfortable.

As they went further they saw a boat sinking, and Moses said, "Master, that boat is sinking, it is going down." The master again ordered him to be quiet; so then Moses was quiet, but he was still most uncomfortable.

When they arrived home, he said, "Master, I would have thought that you would save that little innocent child from drowning, and that you would save that boat which was going down in the water. But you did nothing. I cannot understand; I would like to have an explanation." The master said, "What you saw I saw also. We both saw, so there was no use in your telling me, for I knew. If I had thought that it was better to interfere, I could have done it. Why did you take the trouble to tell me, and spoil your vow of silence?" He continued, "The child who was drowning was going to bring about a conflict between two nations, and thousands and thousands of lives were going to be destroyed in that conflict. When he was drowned this averted the other danger which was to come."

Moses looked at him with great surprise. Then Khidr said, "The boat that was sinking was a boat of pirates, and was sailing to wreck a large ship full of pilgrims and then take what was left in the ship and bring it home. Do you think that you and I can be judge of things? The Judge is behind it. He knows His actions; He knows His work. When you were told to be quiet, it was to keep your lips closed and to observe everything silently, as I was doing."

There is a Persian verse which says, "It is the gardener who knows which plant to rear and which to cut down."

Shall we all take the same attitude? Shall we not go and help others? Yes, you may help them. But at the same time, if a spiritual person does not seem to do what you expect him to do, you do not need to talk about it; for you must know that there is some reason. You do not need to judge him. For the more you evolve the more your reason becomes different. No one has the power to judge another; but one may do one's best oneself.

No doubt at the present time education is a great hindrance to children. They are taught to reason freely with their parents; by reasoning freely, when they come to a certain age, they do not stop to think. Before they think they argue, they dispute, and ask, "Why not?" "Why?"; and in this way they never get to the heavenly reason. For in order to arrive at that reason a responsive attitude is necessary, not an asserting attitude. What a child learns to do today is to take an aggressive attitude. He imposes his knowledge upon others. By the lack of a responsive attitude he loses his opportunity of ever touching that essence of reason which is the spirit of bodhisattva. This has always been the great difficulty in the lives of evolved souls. What happened with Jesus Christ? In the one place there was earthly reason, in the other there was heavenly reason.

Once I looked at my murshid and there came to my inquisitive mind a thought, "Why should a great soul such as my murshid wear gold-embroidered slippers?" But I checked myself at once, and it was only a thought. It could never have escaped my lips; it was under control. But there it was known. I could not cover my insolence with my lips; my heart was open before my murshid as an open book. He instantly saw into it and read my thought. And do you know what answer he gave me? He said, "The treasures of the earth I have at my feet."

Once a murshid had been to the city, and on his return he said, "Oh, I am filled with joy, I am filled with joy. There was such an exaltation in the presence of the Beloved." Then his mureed thought, "There was a beloved and an exaltation; how wonderful! I must go and see if I cannot find one also."

He went through the city, and he came back and said, "Horrible! How terrible the world is! All seem to be at one another's throats; that was the picture I saw. I felt nothing but depression, as if my whole being was torn to pieces." "Yes," the murshid said, "you are right." But explain to me," the mureed said, "why you are so exalted after going out, and why I am so torn to pieces. I cannot bear it; it is horrible." The murshid said, "You did not walk in the rhythm that I walked in through the city."

It is not only the slow rhythm of the walk but the rhythm with which the mind is moving: it is that rhythm with which the observation is gained which makes the difference between one person and another; it is that which brings about the harmony between one person and another.

The person who says, "I will not listen to your reason," no doubt has a reason, as everybody has a reason. But he could have a better reason still if he were able to listen and to understand the reason of another. The reason of a person's mind is just like making circles. One person's mind makes a circle in a minute; another person's mind makes a circle in five minutes: the reason is different. Another person's mind makes a circle in fifteen minutes; his reason is different again. The longer it takes, the wider is the horizon of his vision; and so is his outlook on life.

Reasoning is a ladder. By this ladder one can rise, and from this ladder one may fall. For if one does not go upward by reasoning, then it will help one to go downward; because if for every step one takes upward there is a reason, so there is a reason for every step downward. No doubt this distinction is made to enable one to understand that there is one reason; in reality it is one faculty. One may divide the human body into three parts, but at the same time it is one body, it is one person. Nevertheless, reason is a great factor and has the possibility in it of every curse and of every blessing.

CHAPTER 9
Memory

The work of memory is not creative but perceptive: to receive impressions and to gather them together. Some scientists say that the cells of the brain are impressed by every impression that comes through the senses, and it is that which is kept in the brain, to be brought forth when one wants them. But it is not like that, although this can be taken as a symbolic explanation. The scientist has pictured it as it is in the inner plane, but because he does not recognize the inner plane he wants to explain it in physical terms, and calls it brain cells. This is true in essence; but it is not in the brain, it is in the mind.

Memory is a recording machine which records all that falls upon it through the five senses. What one sees, hears, smells, touches, tastes is recorded upon the memory. A form, a picture, an image, once seen, sometimes remains in the memory for the whole life if it is well recorded by the memory. In the life of the world one hears so many words during the day, and yet some words which the memory has recorded remain for the whole life, as living as ever. So it is with music. Once a person has heard wonderful music and it is recorded in his mind, it remains forever and ever. Memory is such a living machine that you can produce that record at any time; it is there. A good perfume once experienced, once perceived, is remembered; the feeling of taste remains; the feeling of touch memory holds.

Things do not remain in the memory as in a notebook, for as the notebook is dead, so what remains in the notebook is dead. But memory is living, and so what remains in the memory is living also, and has a living sensation. A record of pleasant memory is sometimes so precious that one wishes to sacrifice this objective world for such a record. I was very touched once by seeing a widow whose relations wished me to tell her to go into society, to mix with people, to live a more worldly life. I went to advise her on that subject. But she told me gently, ''All the experiences of this world's life, however pleasant, do not afford me pleasure. My only joy is the memory of my beloved: other things give me unhappiness, other things make me miserable. If I find joy, it is in the thought of my beloved.'' I could not say one word to change her mind. I thought it would be a sin on my part to take her away from her joy. If the memory had been a misery for her, I would have spoken to her otherwise, but it was a happiness for her, the only happiness. I thought that here was the living *sati* (sacrificed widow). I had only a great esteem for her, and could not speak one word.

In memory the secret of heaven and hell is to be found. What is heaven or hell? Where is it? It is only in the memory. Therefore memory is not a small thing. It is not something which is hidden in the brain: it is living, and it is a world in itself.

But people might ask, ''What is wrong, then, if a person has lost his memory? Is it caused by a disorder in the brain?'' In the first place no one really loses his memory. A person may lose his memory, but it does not lose him, because the memory is one's own being. What happens is that a disorder of the brain makes it incapable of distinguishing what the memory contains.

Therefore a person who has lost his memory owing to a disorder still has a memory just the same, and that memory will become clearer to him after death. For the mind is quite distinct from the body; it is something apart, standing independent of the body. The mind is dependent on the body for perceiving the outer experiences which it takes in through the senses, but it is independent of the body for the treasures which it has collected through the outer world.

As we are accustomed to experience everything through the vehicle of this body, even our feelings, this makes us dependent for some time upon the body; but it does not mean that we cannot experience all that belongs to the mind without the help of the body. If a person lifted himself from his objective being, he would find his memory intact. The memory cannot function in the brain which is out of order, but impressions are still recorded during the time that a person has lost his memory; they come back later on. Only, at the time when a person has lost his memory, the memory is not actively making a record of things given to it.

To have a good memory is not only a good thing; it is a bliss. It is a sign of spirituality because it shows that the light of the intelligence is clear and is illuminating every particle of the brain. A good memory is a sign of great souls. Besides, memory is the treasure where one's knowledge has been stored. If a person cannot draw the knowledge he has collected from his memory, then his dependence upon the book is of little worth.

No doubt we always write on paper things belonging to the earth, figures and other facts; but things pertaining to the spiritual order of things, to the divine law, are of much greater importance. The notebook is not made for them; it is in the memory they must be treasured. For memory is not only a recording machine; it is at the same time a fertile ground, and what is put there is continually creative, it is doing something there. Therefore you possess not only what you have deposited;

there is its interest also.

But at the same time we learn in the Sufi path how to erase from the record a living memory of something in the past. That is the work which we accomplish by concentration and meditation. It is not an easy thing; it is the most difficult, but also the most valuable, thing there is. This is why we keep our teachings free from speculations, beliefs, doctrines, and dogmas, for we believe in actual work with ourselves. What if you were told a thing one day and you believed it, and the next day you doubted and did not believe it? If you were told there is a house and a palace in the seventh heaven, what would it do for you? It would only answer your curiosity; it would take you nowhere. It is therefore that we attain to these things by the way of meditation. We can erase from the memory what we wish to, and in this way we are able to make our heaven ourselves. The whole secret of esotericism lies in controlling the mind and in working with it as an artist would work on a canvas to produce whatever he likes.

How can one destroy undesirable thoughts? Must they always be destroyed by the one who has created them? Yes, it is the creator of the thought who must destroy it; and it is not in every person's power to do so. Yet the mind which has reached mastery, which can create as it wishes, can also destroy. When we are able to produce on the canvas of our heart all that we wish and to erase all we wish, then we arrive at that mastery for which our soul craves; we fulfill that purpose for which we are here. Then we become the masters of our destiny. It is difficult, but that is the object that we pursue in life.

Sometimes memory is weakened by too great a strain upon it. When one tries to remember, it puts a strain upon something which is natural. It is the nature of memory to remember, but when you put a strain upon it—"You must remember"—then it will forget. The very fact that you have strained it will make it forget.

One must not try to impress one's mind more deeply than it naturally becomes impressed. It is not necessary to use the brain when trying to remember something, because by using the brain one only strains it. The memory is at your command. If you want to know about something, without your straining the brain it must come instantly. It is an automatic machine; it must bring before you instantly all that you wish to know. If it does not work in that way, there is something wrong with it.

Certainly association of ideas helps. It is just as when a person has lost the thought of the horse from his mind, and the stable reminds him. Your attention is quite enough; will power must not be used to remember things. It is a wrong method that people are applying at present when they say that in order to remember things one must will it. By willing, one weakens. Besides this, a balance between activity and repose is necessary.

Memory is never lost. What happens is that when the mind is upset the memory becomes blurred, because it is the stillness of mind which makes one capable of distinguishing all that one's memory contains. When the mind is upset, when a person is not tranquil, then naturally he is not able to read all that the memory has recorded. It is not true that memory gives away what is stored in it. It is only that man loses the rhythm of life by over-excitement, nervousness, weakness of nerves, anxiety, worry, fear, confusion. It is that which causes a kind of turmoil in the mind, and one cannot distinctly feel things which have once been recorded in the memory. For instance, a person who cannot easily learn by heart must make his mind tranquil as the first thing in order to better his condition. That is the mental way. A physical way of making the memory better is to eat less and sleep normally, not work too much, not worry very much, and to keep all anxiety and fear away. One need not work with memory in order to make it clear. What is required is to make oneself tranquil, rhythmical, and peaceful in order to make memory distinct.

There is a still deeper sphere to which our memory is linked, and that sphere is the universal memory—in other words the divine mind—where we do not only recollect what we have seen or heard or known, but where we can even touch something we have never learned or heard, known or seen. This can be found there also; only for this, the doors of memory should be laid open.

CHAPTER 10

The Heart

A most important aspect of the mind is feeling. If this faculty is not open, then however wise and clever a person may be he is incomplete, he is not living. Mind begins to live from the moment that feeling is wakened in it. Many use the word feeling, but few of us know it. And the more one knows it, the less one speaks of it. It is so vast that if there is any sign of God it is in feeling. Feeling is vibration, and the heart is its vehicle.

When one asks, "What is the heart? Where is the heart?" the answer usually is that heart is in the breast. This is true; there is a nerve center in the breast of man which is so sensitive to our feelings that it is always regarded as the heart. When a person feels a great joy it is in that center that he feels something lighting up, and through the lighting of that center his whole being seems light; he feels as if he were flying. And if depression or despair has come into his life it has an effect upon that center. A man feels his throat choked, and his breath is laden as with a heavy load.

But the heart is not only that. To understand this one should picture a mirror before the heart, focused upon it so that every thing and every feeling is reflected in this mirror, which is in the physical being of man. Just as man is ignorant of his soul, so he does not know where his heart is, nor where the center is where his feelings are reflected. It is a fact known to scientists that when a child is formed it begins from the heart. But the mystic's conception is that the heart, which is the beginning of form, is also the beginning of the spirit which makes man an individual. The depth of that spirit is in reality what we call the heart. Through this we understand that there is such a thing as a heart, which is the deepest depth of man's being.

In these days people attribute less importance to sentiment and rely more upon the intellect. The reason for this is that when they meet the two kinds of people, the intellectual and the sentimental, they find greater balance in the intellectual man than in the one with much sentiment. This is no doubt true; but the very reason for the lack of balance is that there is a greater power than the intellect, and that power is sentiment. The earth is fruitful, yet not as powerful as the water. The intellect is creative, yet not as powerful as the heart and the sentiment. In reality the intellectual man will also prove unbalanced in the end if he has no sentimental side to his being. Are there not many people of whom one can say, "I like him, love him, admire him, but he closes his heart?" The one who closes his heart neither loves others completely nor allows others to love him fully. Besides, a man who is only intellectual in time becomes skeptical, doubting, unbelieving, and destructive, since there is no power of the heart to balance the intellect.

The Sufi considers the devotion of the heart to be the best thing to cultivate for spiritual realization. Many people may not agree, but it is a fact that the one who closes his heart to his fellow man closes his heart to God. Jesus Christ did not say,

"God is the intellect," he said, "God is love." Therefore, if the peace of God can be found anywhere, it is not in any church on earth nor in heaven above, but in the heart of man. The place where one is most certain to find God is in the loving heart of a kind man.

Many people believe that by the help of reason man will act according to a certain standard of morals, but it is not reason that makes people good; and even if they seem good or righteous, they are only made so artificially. The prisoners in jail can all seem righteous. But if natural goodness and righteousness can be found anywhere, it is in the spring of the heart from which life rises; and every drop of this spring is a living virtue. This proves that goodness is not manmade; it is man's very being. And if he lacks goodness it is not through lack of training —although training is often most desirable—but because he has not yet found his true self. Goodness is natural, for a normal person is necessarily good. No one needs teaching in order to live a good or a righteous life. If love is the torch on a person's path, it shows him what fairness means, and the honor of his word, charity of heart, and righteousness. Do we not sometimes see a young man who, with all his boisterous tendencies, suddenly finds a girl whom he begins to love, and who when he really loves her begins to show a change in his life? He becomes gentle, for he must train himself for her sake; he does without things he was never before willing to give up. And in the same way, where there is love forgiveness is not very difficult. A child comes to its mother, even after having offended a thousand times, and asks her forgiveness. There is no one else to go to. And it does not take a moment for the mother's heart to forgive. Forgiveness was waiting there to manifest itself.

One cannot help being kind when there is feeling. Someone whose feeling goes out to another person sees when that person needs his feeling, and he strikes a note of sympathy in everyone he meets, finding the point of contact in every soul because he has love. There are people who say, "But is it not unwise to give oneself to everyone in unrestrained tenderness, as people in general are not trustworthy?" But if a person is good and kind, this goodness ought to become manifest to everyone, and the doors of the heart should be closed to nobody.

Jesus Christ not only told us to love our friends; he went as far as to say we should love our enemies. The Sufi treads the same path. He considers charity of heart towards his fellow man to be love for God; and in showing love to everyone, he feels he is giving his love to God. Here the Sufi and the yogi differ. The yogi is not unkind, but he says, "I love you all, but I had better keep away from you, for your souls are always groping in darkness, and my soul is in the light. Your friendship will harm my soul, so I had better love you from afar." The Sufi says, "It is a trial, but it should be tried. I shall take up my everyday duties as they come along." Although he knows how unimportant the things of the world are and does not overvalue them, he attends to his responsibilities towards those who love him, like him, depend upon him, follow him; and he tries to find the best way of coming to terms with all those who dislike and despise him. He lives in the world, and yet he is not of the world. In this way the Sufi considers that the main principle in the fulfillment of the purpose of his life is to love man.

Those who love their enemies and yet lack patience are like a burning lantern with little oil. It cannot keep alight, and in the end the flame fades away. The oil in the path of love is patience, and besides this it is unselfishness and self-sacrifice from beginning to end.

Some say, "I loved dearly once, but I was disappointed." This is as if to say, "I dug in the earth, but when the mud came I was disappointed." It is true that mud came, but with patience one would have reached the water one day. Only patience can endure. Only endurance produces greatness.

Imitation gold can be as beautiful as real gold; the imitation

diamond is as bright as a real diamond. The difference is that
the one fails the test of endurance and the other stands up to it.
Yet man should not be compared with objects. Man has
something divine in him, and he can prove this by his
endurance in the path of love.

Whom then should one love, and how should one love?
Whatever a person loves, whether duty, human beings, art,
friends, an ideal, or his fellow creatures, he has assuredly
opened the door through which he must pass in order to reach
that love which is God. The beginning of love is an excuse; it
leads to that ideal of love which is God alone. Some say that
they can love God but not human beings. But this is like saying
to God, "I love Thee, but not Thine image." Can one hate the
human creatures in which God's image is to be found and yet
claim to love God? If one is not tolerant, not willing to sacrifice,
can one then claim the love of the Lord? The first lesson is the
widening of the heart and the awakening of its inner feeling.
The sign of saintliness is not in the power of words; not in high
position, either spiritual or intellectual; not in magnetism. The
saintly spirit only expresses itself in the love of all creatures; it is
the continuous springing of love from the divine fountain in the
heart of man. When once that fountain is turned on it purifies
the heart. It makes the heart transparent to reveal both the
outer and the inner worlds. The heart becomes the vehicle for
the soul to see all that is within and without. Then one not only
communicates with another person, but also with God.

Part Three:

TRAINING THE MIND

CHAPTER 11

Will Power

Will is not *a* power: it is all the power there is. How did God create the world? By will. Therefore that in us which we call will power is in reality a God power, a power which, by our recognizing its potential, increases and proves to be the greatest phenomenon in life. If there is any secret that can be learned behind the mystery of the world of phenomena, it is will power. It is by will power that all we do, physically or mentally, is accomplished. Our hands, with all their perfect mechanism, cannot hold a glass of water if there is no will power to support them. A person may seem to be healthy, but if will power fails him he will not be able to stand, for it is not the body which makes us stand upright, it is our will power. It is not the strength of the body that makes us move about, it is will power holding the body which makes it move. Therefore in reality birds do not fly with their wings, they fly with will power; fishes do not swim with their bodies, they swim with their will power. And when man has the will to swim, he swims like a fish.

Man has been able to accomplish tremendous things by will power. Success and failure are its phenomena. It is only the phenomenon of will which brings one to success; and when will fails, however qualified and intelligent a person may be, he fails. Therefore will is not a human power, it is a divine power in man. Its work with the mind is still greater than that with the body, for no man can hold a thought in his mind for a moment if there is not the strength of will to hold it. If a person cannot concentrate, cannot keep his thought still for a moment, it means that will power has failed him.

Now coming to the question of what will power is made of. In poetical words will power is love; in metaphysical terms love is will power. If one says God is love, it really means God is will; for the love God manifests after the creation, but the will of God caused the creation. Therefore the original aspect of love is will. For instance, the Taj Mahal is said to be the token of the love that an emperor had for his beloved. But when one looks at it objectively, one cannot call it an expression of love; one would sooner call it a phenomenon of will. For the beginning of the building at least, one may look at the spirit, the impulse which started it, as a phenomenon of the emperor's will; one can say that after it was finished it was the expression of his love. When a person says, "I desire it," "I wish it," it is an incomplete will, a will which is not conscious of its strength, a will which is not sure what it wills. But when he says, "I will it," that means it is definite. A person who never can say, "I will it," has no will.

From this we may conclude that will is the source and the origin of all phenomena. The will is the action of the soul. One can also call the soul the self of the will. The difference between will and soul is like the difference between a person and his action.

Will and consciousness are fundamentally the same. It is the two expressions of one thing which makes them distinct; this duality comes out of unity. It is God's own being that in expression is will, in response consciousness. In other words, in action it is will, in stillness it is consciousness, just as fundamentally sound and light are one and the same thing, which in one condition produces light through the friction of vibrations, while in another condition the same vibrations are audible. This is why the nature and character of sound and light are one. And so are the nature and character of consciousness and will, because both things belong to God's own being.

The Qur'an says, "We said, 'Be,' and it became." This is a key to the world of phenomena. To the progressive mind, to the advanced thought, this shows that manifestation came into existence in answer to that will which expressed itself in saying, "Be." This phenomenon belongs not only to the origin of things; it belongs to the whole being of things, to the whole process of manifestation.

We are apt to look at this creation as a mechanism, as man today looks at it, and we do not stop to think how a mechanism can exist without an engineer. What is a mechanism? It is only an expression of the will of the engineer, an engineer who made it for his convenience. But as we do not see the engineer before us and see only the mechanism, we involve ourselves in the laws of its working and forget the engineer by whose command the whole mechanism is going on. As the great inspirer and philosopher Rumi says in his *Masnavi*, "The earth, water, fire, air, these seem to us like things or objects; but before God they are living beings. They stand as His obedient servants, and they obey the divine will." A part of that will we inherit as our own divine heritage, and it is our consciousness of it which makes it greater; if we are not conscious of it, it becomes smaller.

It is the optimistic attitude towards life which develops will; the pessimistic attitude reduces it, robs it of its great power. Therefore if there is anything that hinders our progress in life, it is our own selves. It is proved a thousand times over that there is no one in the world who can be a worse enemy to us than ourselves, for in every failure we see ourselves to be standing in our own light.

The earth holds the seed, and the result is that a plant springs out of it. And so it is with the heart: the heart holds the seed of thought, and there also a plant springs up and brings the fruit of fulfillment. But it is not only the thought but the power of holding the thought which is of very great importance. Therefore the factor of the heart, which holds the thought, is very important for the fulfillment of life's purpose. Often a person says, "I try my best, but I cannot concentrate my mind; I cannot make my mind still." That is true; but it is not true that he tries his best. Best does not end there; best really brings the purpose to its fulfillment.

The mind is just like a restive horse. Bring a wild horse and yoke it to a carriage; it is such a strange experience for it that it will kick, jump, run, and try to destroy the carriage. And so it is a weight for the mind to carry when you make it take one thought and hold that thought for a while. It becomes restive because it is not accustomed to discipline. The mind by itself will hold a thought; the mind will hold so fast to a thought of disappointment, pain, or grief, to a sorrow or a failure, that you cannot take away from its grip that which it holds. But when you ask the mind to hold a particular thought, then it says, "I will not hold it." When once the mind is disciplined by concentration, by the power of will, then it becomes your servant. And once the mind has become your servant, what more do you wish? Then your mind is your own; you are the king of your kingdom.

One might ask why we should not let the mind be free also, as we are free. But we and the mind are not two things, so it would be like saying, "Let the horse be free and the rider be free." Then the horse would want to go to the south and the rider would want to go to the north. How can they go together? There are even people who would say, "Let us be free, and let the will be free.'' But what are we then? We are nothing. Discipline has a place in man's life. And self-discipline, however difficult and tyrannical it might seem to us in the beginning, yet is that which in the end makes the soul the master of self. It was not in vain that the great sages and adepts led an ascetic life; there was a purpose in it. This is not something to follow, but it should be understood what use they made of it, what they accomplished by it. It was self-discipline, the development of will power.

All the lack that we find in life is the lack of will, and all the blessing that comes to us comes by the power of will. Some think that will power does not depend on ourselves, that it is given to some as a grace, as a blessing. It does not depend on ourselves, but it is ourselves. It is grace and blessing no doubt, but at the same time it is to be found in ourselves: it is our very being.

DEVELOPING THE WILL

The nature of the life we live is to rob us of our will. Not only the struggle we have to undergo in life, but also our own self, our thoughts, our desires, our wishes, our motives weaken our will. The person who knows how our inner being is connected with the perfect will will find that what makes the will smaller, narrower, more limited, is our experience throughout life. Our joys rob us of our will as do our sorrows; our pleasures rob us of our will as do our pains. The only way of maintaining the power of will is by studying the existence of will and by analyzing what among all the things in ourselves is will.

It might seem that motive increases will power, but in the end we will find that it robs us of will power. Motive is a shadow upon the intelligence, although the higher the motive the higher the soul, and the greater the motive the greater the man. When the motive is beneath the ideal it is the fall of man, and when his motive is his ideal it is his rise. According to the width of motive man's vision is wide, and according to the power of motive man's strength is great.

There is a saying, "Man proposes, God disposes." One is always faced with a power greater than oneself which does not always support one's desire. And naturally a person with will, faced with a greater power, must sooner or later give in and be impressed by the loss of his own will. This is one example, but a hundred examples could be given to show how one is robbed of one's will without realizing it. Very often a person thinks that by being active or determined he maintains his will, and that by being passive he loses his will. But it is not so. Where there is a battle there is an advance and there is a retreat. By a retreat one is not defeated, and by an advance one does not always succeed. A person who exerts his will all the time strains it and exhausts it very soon. It is like being too sure of a string that one has in one's hand while rubbing it on the edge of a sharp stone. Very often one sees that people who profess great will power fail much sooner than those who do not profess it.

There is also always a battle between will power and wisdom; and the first and wisest thing to do is to bring about a harmony between them. When a person says, "I wish to do this; I will do this," and at the same time his sense says, "No, you cannot do it; you must not do it," then even with all his will power either he cannot do it or he will do something against his better judgment.

This also shows us life in another light: that those who are wise but without will are as helpless as those with will power but without wisdom. There is no use keeping wisdom at the front and will power at the back; nor is there any use in keeping will power at the front and wisdom at the back. What is necessary is to make the two as one, and this can be done by becoming conscious of the action of both in all one does. At the same time one can practice it in one's everyday life by depriving oneself of things one likes. If a person always has what he wants, no doubt he spoils his will, for then his will has no reaction.

A stimulus is given to the will when one deprives oneself of what one desires: then the will becomes conscious of itself, alive; it wonders why it should not have it. For instance, a person wants to have peaches, but at the same time he is very much attracted to the flower of the peach. He thinks the flower is beautiful, and then the idea comes, why not let it remain on the plant? That will make him decide not to pick it. This gives him a stimulus, because first desire wanted to take hold of it, and then sense wanted to work with it. As light comes from friction, so also does will come from friction.

The power of will is in controlling, in contrast with imagination, which works without control, for if one wants to control it one spoils it. Nothing in the world, either in the sphere of the mind or on the physical plane, can move without the power of will; but while with one thing the power of will is in absolute control, with the other it is working automatically.

There is another enemy of will power, and that is the power of desire. Sometimes this robs will power of its strength; sometimes will power becomes strong by a conflict with desire. The self-denial taught in the Bible generally means the crushing of desires. This should not be taken as a principle but as a process. Those who have taken it as a principle have lost; those who have taken it as a process have gained.

The enemy of sense, of wisdom, is the lack of tranquility of mind. When the mind is tranquil it produces the right thought, and wisdom naturally rises as a fountain. The Sufis have therefore taught different exercises, both in physical and in meditative form, to make the mind tranquil, so that the wisdom which is there may spring up as a fountain. It is not in disturbed water that one can see one's image reflected; it is in still water that one sees it clearly. Our heart is likened to water, and when it is still wisdom springs up by itself. It is wisdom and will together that work towards a successful issue.

Will power is systematically developed by first disciplining the body. The body must sit in the prescribed posture; it must stand in the place it is asked to stand in. The body should not become restless, tired, by what is asked of it, but it should answer the demands of the person to whom it belongs. The moment the Sufi begins to discipline the body, he begins to see how undisciplined it always was; then he finds out that this body which he has always called "mine," "myself," and for whose comfort he has always done everything he could, that this infidel seems to be most disobedient, most faithless.

After that comes the discipline of the mind. This is done by concentration. When the mind is thinking of something else and one wishes it to think on one specific thought, then it becomes very restless; it does not want to remain in one spot, for it has always been without discipline. The difficulty starts when one tries to concentrate: it begins to jump, while at other times it only moves about. But the mind is meant to be an obedient servant, just as the body is meant to become an obedient tool with which to experience life. If they are not in order, if they do not act as one wishes them to, then one cannot hope for real happiness, real comfort in life.

The mind can be trained by regarding it as a separate entity, watching it, and teaching it. There is the ego and there is the mind; we should look at the mind and think, "I am the ego; my mind is before me," and then analyze it, imagine it to be an entity, and speak with it, and the answer will come. Even animals are trained; can man not train himself? When one cannot train oneself this only means that one does not want to train oneself. It is laziness, lethargy; one does not want to take the trouble. For instance, very often when asked to read a poem, people will say, "Yes, I shall be glad to read it presently." They do not want to exert their brain. First they do not want to take trouble for another, and then their laziness increases and they may arrive at a state where they do not even want to take trouble for themselves. It begins with selfishness—they do not want to think about another—and then it ends by a person not wanting to think about himself. Then what is he thinking about? Nothing.

One should say to the mind, "Look here, you are my mind, you are my instrument, you are my slave and servant, you are here to help me, to work for me in this world. You have to listen to me. You will do whatever I wish, you will think whatever I wish, you will feel whatever I wish. You will not think or feel differently from my wishes, for you are my mind and you must prove in the end to be mine." By doing this we begin to analyze our mind: we begin to see where it is rusted; whether it has become too cool or overheated. We can train it ourselves, in accordance with its condition; and it is we who are the best trainers of our mind, better than anybody else in the world.

The will can be strengthened by practice: by exerting it to overcome obstacles without and within; by acting contrary to one's inclination; by holding impulses in check, not allowing them to go to the full length of their swing; by refraining from any action or expression to which one may be inclined, not allowing oneself to be overcome by a fit of anger, of laughter, of tears, or by extreme joy or sorrow, or whatever mood, but rather changing the emotion to its opposite (anger to mildness, laughter to sorrow, tears to joy), by checking the emotion and effacing it, or by holding it in our control while yet letting it have its course.

To know when to persist in our own will and when to submit to the will of others is often difficult; and sometimes we think it most difficult to know what is the will of God and what is our own will. Sometimes six months later, sometimes a year or years afterwards, we see clearly what we should have done in a certain case, what course we should have taken; which at the time we could not discern although we tried to. If at the moment of

difficulty we were as calm as we are later, as free from thoughts
of the pleasure, the happiness, the discomfort, or the loss that
would result to ourselves from our action, we should see as
clearly in that moment and perceive plainly the will of God.

The will can become so strong that it controls the body,
making it perfectly healthy. But, one may ask, then what about
death? Death is not something foreign to will power; even it is
caused by will power. One thinks one does not invite one's
death. Indeed, one does not, but the personal will becomes
feeble and the greater will impresses this feeble will, turning it
into itself. For the smaller will belongs to the greater will. Sufis
call the former *kadr* and the latter *kaza*. Kaza reflects upon kadr
its command, and kadr unconsciously accepts it. On the surface
a man may still want to live, but in the depth he has resigned
himself to die. If man did not resign himself to death before his
life is taken away from him, he would not die.

Resignation of the human will to the divine will is the real
crucifixion. After that crucifixion follows resurrection. One can
come to this by seeking the pleasure of God; and it is not
difficult, once one has begun to seek His pleasure. It is only
when one does not begin to try that one does not know what is
the pleasure of God. But apart from this there is another lesson
which the Sufis have taught: to seek the pleasure of one's fellow
men. This is the very thing that man usually refuses to do. He is
quite willing to do the pleasure of God, but when one asks him
to seek the pleasure of his fellow men he refuses.

In either case, however, one is seeking the pleasure of one and
the same Being. One begins with resignation; but when one has
learned to be resigned in life, and when one is tuned to the
divine will, one does not need to be resigned, for one's wish
becomes the divine impulse.

CHAPTER 12

Concentration

To gain knowledge of concentration requires not only study but also balance. Before touching this subject I would like to explain what motive we have behind concentration. There are two aspects of life: the audible life and the silent life. By audible life I mean all sensations that we experience through our five senses. This is distinct from the life which I would call the silent life. When one asks what benefit one derives from getting in touch with the silent life, the anwer is that the benefit is as abstract as the silent life itself. The life of sensation is clear; its benefit is clear; and yet as limited as is the life of sensation, so limited is its benefit. That is why in the end we find all our experiences of little value. Their importance lasts as long as we experience them, but after that the importance of the life of sensation is finished.

The value of the silent life is independent. We are inclined to attach a value to something which concerns our outer life. The silent life does not give us a special benefit but a general benefit. In other words, if there is a minor wound on the body an external application of a certain medicament can cure it; but there are other medicines which can cure the general condition, and this is more satisfactory than the external cure, though it is less spectacular.

One cannot say exactly what profit is gained by concentration, but in reality every kind of profit is to be attained through it, in all directions. There are two kinds of concentration: automatic and intentional. Automatic concentration is found in many people who do not know that they concentrate and yet do. They concentrate automatically, some to their disadvantage, some to their advantage. Those who concentrate to their advantage are the ones whose mind is fixed on their business, on their art, on any occupation they have. They are the ones who because of their concentration can work more successfully; according to a person's power of concentration, so will be his success.

* I once had the pleasure of hearing Paderewski in his own house. He began to play gently on his piano. Every note took him into a deeper and deeper ocean of music. Any meditative person could see clearly that he was so concentrated in what he did that he knew not where he was. The works of great composers which will always live, which win the hearts of men, whence do they come? From concentration. So it is with a poet, so it is with an artist; it is concentration which brings color and line, which makes a picture. Naturally, whether one is an artist or a writer, a musician or a poet, in business or industry, in the absence of concentration one can never succeed.

Sometimes concentration works to one's disadvantage. There are some people who always think that they are unlucky, that everything they do will go wrong, that everybody dislikes them, that everybody hates them. Some begin to think that they are unable to do anything, that they are incapable, useless. Others out of self-pity think that they are ill. In that way even if they are not ill they create illness. Some by concentration cherish illness, always think of it. No physician could be successful with them. An old physician once said, "There are many diseases, but there are many more patients." Once a person has become a patient through concentration, he is difficult to cure. And there are many such cases of automatic concentration to the disadvantage of man.

Intentional concentration is taught by thinkers, philosophers, and meditative people. The whole of mysticism, of esotericism, is based upon the idea of concentration. This mystical concentration can be divided into four different grades. The first is concentration, the next contemplation, the third meditation, the fourth realization.

The first grade is the fixing of one's thought upon one object. One should not concentrate upon just any object that comes along, for what one concentrates upon has an effect upon one. When one concentrates on a dead object it has the effect of deadening the soul; when one concentrates on a living object it naturally has a living effect. The secret of the teachings of all prophets and mystics is to be found in this.

This concentration is achieved in three different ways. The first way is by action. One makes a certain movement or performs an action which helps the mind to concentrate on a certain object. Another way is with the help of words. By the repetition of certain words one learns to think automatically of a certain object. The third way is with the help of memory. Memory is like a builder's yard. From this the builder takes anything he likes; tiles, pillars, bricks, whatever he wants. The man who concentrates in this way does the same as children who have bricks to build toy houses with. He collects things in his memory, and with them he composes objects in order to concentrate on what he wishes.

As to contemplation, it is only when a person is advanced enough that he can contemplate, because contemplation is not on an object, it is on an idea. No doubt a man may think that he is ready to do anything, and that after concentration he can contemplate; but the nature of the mind is such that it slips out of one's hands the moment one tries to hold it. Therefore before one really starts to think the mind has already thrown off the object of concentration like a restive horse. Mind is not always so unruly; it proves to be unruly when it wants to rule itself. It is like the body: one may feel restful sitting naturally, but as soon as one keeps quite still for five minutes, the body begins to feel restless. And it is still more difficult to make the mind obey. Mystics therefore find a rope to tie the mind in a certain place where it cannot move. What is that rope? That rope is breath. It is by that rope that they bind the mind and make it stand where they wish it to stand. It is like the bird which uses its saliva to make its nest; so the mystic out of breath creates atmosphere, creates light and magnetism in which to live.

One characteristic of the mind is that it is like a gramophone record: whatever is impressed upon it, it is able to reproduce. Another characteristic is that it not only reproduces something, but it creates what is impressed upon it. If ugliness is recorded, it will produce disagreement, inharmony. The learning of concentration clears the record and makes it produce what we like, not what comes automatically. In this world one is so open to impressions; one goes about with the eyes and ears open. But it is not only the eyes, not only the ears which are open: the lips are open to give out what the eyes and ears take in, and that is the dangerous part.

The third part of concentration is meditation. In this grade one becomes communicative. One communicates with the silent life, and naturally a communication opens up with the outer life also. It is then that a man starts to realize that both the outer and the inner life, in fact everything, is communicative. Then he begins to learn what can never be learned by study or from books: that the silent life is the greatest teacher and knows all things. It not only teaches, but it gives that peace, that joy, that power and harmony which make life beautiful.

No one can claim to be meditative. For a meditative person need not say it with the lips. His atmosphere says so, and it is the atmosphere alone which can say whether it is true or false. Once I asked my spiritual teacher what was the sign of knowing God. He said, "Not those who call out the name of God, but those whose silence says it." Many go about looking, searching for something worthwhile, something wonderful, but there is nothing more wonderful than the soul of man.

Realization is the result of the three other grades. In the third kind of experience man pursued meditation; but in this grade, meditation pursues man. In other words, it is no longer the singer who sings the song, but the song sings the singer. This fourth grade is a kind of expansion of consciousness; it is the unfoldment of the soul; it is diving deep within oneself; it is communicating with each atom of life existing in the whole world; it is realizing the real I in which is the fulfillment of life's purpose.

MYSTICAL CONCENTRATION

Vibrations are that which becomes audible, and atoms are that which becomes visible. There are two kinds of vibrations, fine and gross, and there are two kinds of atoms, which are also fine and gross. Fine vibrations are not perceived by the ears but by the sense of perception. These are the vibrations of feeling, which convey to us our sorrow and joy, and also convey them to another to a certain extent. The fine atoms are not seen by our eyes but by the sense of perception. Grouping together, these form thought. The grosser vibrations are those of sound and voice which our material ears hear, and the grosser atoms are the atoms which form the substance which our eyes can see.

By concentration is meant the grouping together of the fine

atoms on the model of the objects seen by our external eyes so as to form upon our mind a picture of objects as is seen by our eyes in the external world. It is difficult at first, because the mind has never been controlled, and therefore it is not accustomed to obey. It becomes tired when holding any thought grouped of fine atoms. But when feeling is holding the thought, then it is held fast, even against desire. For the atom is the outcome of vibration, and when the vibration holds it, the atom is held like steel with a magnet. Therefore concentration is developed by holding an object by the help of feeling. In this is the mystery of all devotion.

The will plays the most important part in concentration. Its work is first to collect the atoms from the storehouse of memory, and next to hold them together, making one single vision to be concentrated on. It is therefore that the strong-willed can concentrate better than the weak-willed. Those who accomplish great works and difficult works and those who are successful in every enterprise they take up are the possessors of a strong will. Will develops concentration, and concentration develops the will. People who are changeable, who go from one thought to another, show lack of will as well as lack of concentration.

Every person, whether acquainted with mystical things or not, naturally has the faculty to concentrate to a lesser or a greater degree. Of course one develops the faculty by exercise, and by not making use of the faculty one weakens it. It is little known to the world, but it is a great secret understood and practiced by the mystics, that if the will is able to collect atoms from the memory and construct an intended vision and to hold it, in time it becomes capable of mastering all affairs in the world, however difficult they may be. When perfection in this is reached, one has attained the power of miracle: that which is impossible for the world is possible for such a one.

Concentration may be considered of three kinds. The first is visualizing a form; the second is thinking of a name, the form of which is not distinct; the third is the thought of an attribute which is beyond name and form. The one who has not mastered concentration on form in its full extent must not try the second kind; and after trying the second kind of concentration thoroughly, one may try the third. Lack in the first concentration will continue in the second and third grades; therefore the first must be well mastered.

There are three different sorts in the first kind of concentration: visualizing the form of an object; looking into the details of the form; and visualizing a multitude of forms at the same time.

There are three sorts in the concentration on a name too. The first sort is holding the name of a person or object unknown to one in the mind and forming it by one's imagination. The second sort is retaining the name of a known person or object in the mind with the memory of the same. The third is holding the name of an entity that is difficult to imagine, that is beyond the reach of the eyes or mind.

In concentration on the attribute also there are three sorts. The first is on the natural feelings, such as kindness, goodness, amiability, or bitterness. The second sort is on wealth, power, position, or magnetism. And the third sort is on intuition, inspiration, blessing, illumination.

A gradual progress, step by step, is advisable in concentration, which should be carried on with strength, courage, and patience.

The first step to concentration is observation. The one who lacks observation cannot concentrate well. Observation depends upon steadiness of mind, and this steadiness can be brought about by interest. Those who have no interest in anything or anybody have no steadiness of mind, and those whose mind is not steady cannot observe properly. Concentration on the spiritual teacher, practiced among the Hindus and the Sufis both, teach this secret.

As long a time as a person observes an object, so long in proportion its memory lasts and will come before the eye of his perception anytime he wishes. When we think of a certain thing and cannot recall it to our memory, either our mind is unsteady at that time or there was lack of observation of the object when we saw it. There is no better way of cultivating one's memory than by the observation of a single object at a certain time. The observant show by their very looks a powerful will, a steady mind, and a capacity for concentration.

Every object that the eyes have once seen is stored more or less deep in one's memory, but it in time scatters to pieces. When one remembers it, one gathers by the power of the will the pieces that were once scattered, making it whole.

The question arises, what makes the object scattered? The answer is that shadows of the other objects we see and store in the mind fall upon the object, cutting it to pieces. And yet the pieces of every object remain close together; it is the affinity between the pieces that holds them. Man groups them by the power of his will and by the light of intelligence in his waking state. In a dream he sometimes cannot group them properly, for the light of intelligence is dim and the power of the will is feeble. Therefore one sometimes sees a lion with an eagle's wings or a man with the ears of an elephant. All things seen and unseen that man sees in his dreams are pieces of more than one object thus joining together, owing to the lack of will and intelligence.

Concentration is much more important than any other activity in life, for it is neither activity nor repose, and yet it is both. It is activity in the sense that one creates and constructs the object of concentration; and it is repose in the sense that while one holds the object on which one is concentrating one controls by repose the further activity of the mind. One is like a rider holding his horse for a moment when it is standing on its hind legs, which is activity and at the same time repose.

Concentration may be divided into three stages: command, activity, and control. First, the will commands the mind to become active and create the desired object. Next, the mind immediately carries out this command by constructing the desired object according to its capability. And thirdly, the will holds the further activity of the mind as a master rider would hold the reins of his horse, to prevent it from taking any further steps from the place where he desires it to stop.

The great hindrance that stands against concentration is the thought of one's own being. When one thinks of one's own presence and at the same time thinks, ''I am concentrating on a certain object,'' it is impossible to have full concentration. The more one loses the thought of one's own being from one's consciousness, the more one becomes capable of concentration. As self-consciousness is the enemy of a speaker, singer, doctor, or lawyer, so it is the great enemy of the one who concentrates. Concentration is practiced to avoid self-consciousness, and self-consciousness is the only thing that keeps one from progress. The Sufi, while concentrating, uses abstinence against the constant and uncontrollable activity of the mind.

Sometimes one pictures an object in one's mind's eye and sees it, after a time, standing before one in reality. The more concentration of mind a person has, the more he has this experience. I recall things that I had once pictured in my mind coming to reality even twelve years later.

A person wonders whether it is concentration that made a

thing happen in the course of time, or whether concentration perceived beforehand what was going to come. The fact is that both things are right. For instance, a person was thinking of buying a diamond of a certain shape, a certain kind. Perhaps he thought strongly or deeply of this for some time. And five years later, when he had already forgotten about it, somebody presented him with a diamond ring.

The question whether his concentration made the diamond for him and made the friend give it to him or whether he saw the diamond in his concentration because it was to be given may be answered thus: no doubt there was a diamond in store for him, waiting to be on his finger someday, which was his portion in life. But at the same time the fact of his thinking strongly about it made the diamond come straight to him, without going, perhaps, into the possession of many, and without his striving more for it.

Although concentration helps in foreseeing things, yet it is not concentration but foresight that aids. Therefore a thought of this kind need not be a man's own thought, though at the moment it seems to be. Really speaking, it should be called a vision or an intuition, the former if it occurs in sleep, the latter if in the waking state.

Concentration has the power of creating things. It can bring things that were not meant to be for a person, it can create things which otherwise the person might never have. In short, the master of concentration can raise himself from earth to heaven, can turn a miserable person into a most happy one, and can make a person who always has failures successful.

The Persian poet Hafiz says, "Befool not yourself, seeing the ragged sleeves of a dervish, for under this ragged sleeve a most powerful arm is hidden."

As the sun has its rising, zenith, and setting, so the mind has three states, called by the Sufi *uruj, kemal,* and *zaval,* which come alternately.

Uruj is that state of mind in which a person thinks with energy and enthusiasm, "I am going to do such and such a thing." In order to create its object this state of mind produces such a force and power that in its excess it produces a mist that often dims the faculty of reason and justice.

The state of mind which is kemal is perceived during that time when an action is being performed. The mist which the energy of mind has produced reaches, in kemal, its culmination, which is the end of the joy or sorrow pertaining to the deed, because the excess of force becomes exhausted.

Zaval is that state of mind in which the power of enthusiasm is lost and the joy and sorrow of the deed are past, but the memory remains. If the impression is sorrowful, needles prick through the sore of the wounded heart; if it is joyous, a tickling and uplifting feeling is perceived. These feelings diminish and vanish in time in the entire assimilation in the essence.

The master of concentration is he who produces at will not only uruj but kemal and zaval also. He attains self-mastery, when both sin and virtue bow at his feet. It is he who may sneer at the pleasures of heaven and jeer at the tortures of hell.

The secret of continuing uruj is known to the mystics, and it is their refraining from indulging in uruj. For instance, if a dish be delicious, a greedy person will eat it all the faster; but a person who wishes really to enjoy the dish must eat more slowly. A greedy person would take a fragrant flower and wish to smell it in one moment. The next moment he may not have the desire to sense and enjoy it, and the flower will have lost its fragrance.

If one studies this secret in all aspects of life, one can enjoy life and can make even the passing joys of life stable to a certain extent. This is a thing which every soul desires, but none can accomplish it save a mystic, who by patience and perseverance has conquered the self, and by conquering himself has mastered the whole life.

The life of the mystics teaches us; by observing it keenly we can learn many things. Sufis make *khilvat*, seclusion, at a certain time in the day, on a certain day in the week, in a certain week in the month, and in a certain month in the year. The greatest among them have devoted to seclusion a certain period of their life—the early part, or when aged—which they call *gusha nashini*. They have a shawl thrown over the head, keeping the eyes covered from all other objects in order to retain the object of concentration in the mind without any break. The Christian monks and nuns showed in their lives the tendency to seclusion. The veil on the head of the nun covers the eyes from the impressions which may come from the right or left side. The retirement of the yogis also suggests the same tendency for the purpose of concentration.

Busy as we are in our life, with a thousand things in a day, we naturally cannot have a good concentration. But our life needs more effort and seclusion than that of the pious ones who are already on the path. Therefore our first lesson in the way of seclusion should be to practice the principle in our everyday life. When doing work we must try and keep our mind on it, not allowing it to be attracted by anything, however important and attractive it may be. If not, we lose both, as in the story of the dog who went after his reflection in the water with bread in his mouth and lost the piece he had already. If we are thinking of something we must not let another thought, either on our part or on the part of another, break our concentration. When we speak we must not change the subject of our speech in the middle. We should finish one topic, even if it be of less importance. By doing so in thought, speech, and action, we develop our concentration, attending to our daily affairs at the same time.

Single-mindedness as a nature becomes a great help to concentration. People with a great many responsibilities and a great many interests in life cannot keep up single-mindedness, which is indeed a great power. This nature can be developed by concentration, but there are also a great many things in everyday life which help towards its development. The first essential thing for one who practices concentration is to allow one thought at a time or one action at a time, and to keep mind and body busy together. When a person is doing one thing he should not be thinking of another; and if he wishes to think something out he must not be doing something at the same time. Single-mindedness is complete absorption of one's whole being in a single thought, speech, or action.

There is also another side to it. Single-mindedness can be developed by dwelling on a subject until the thought is finished, and while thinking on the subject not allowing the mind to take up something else. The same law should be observed in speech: one must not change the topic in the midst of the speech. The same should be observed in action: one must busy oneself in action without taking up anything else until that action is finished. In this way one can develop concentration at every moment of the day and night. And by acquiring this one acquires mastery over one's own life as well as over life in general.

When a person develops concentration he does not need to make a regular concentration, although a Sufi likes to do so, for his life becomes a concentration. If he is speaking on a certain subject, he does not suddenly change the subject; if he is thinking about something he does not break his thought; and if he is doing something he does not change his mind and leave it half done in order to accomplish something else. He continues at every moment the work he is doing until it is finished. That is the secret of concentration.

A person may practice concentration for a certain time in the day, but if then throughout the day he keeps on changing his mind from one thing to another, he will not be able to

accomplish concentration in a thousand years. Single-mindedness is the secret of concentration. Thereby man improves his
manners. When a man speaking about something begins to say
something else before the subject is finished, it is ill manners
besides lack of concentration.

There is also a possibility that a person with great development in concentration may become the slave of concentration,
so that he may not be able to put out of his mind any thought
that happens to come, to stop humming a tune of which he
himself has grown tired, or to throw off depression because a
depressing thought holds his mind, that mind that is developed
and capable of concentration. The Sufi therefore masters
concentration but does not let concentration master him,
mastery being the only motive that leads to perfection.

Dwelling on a thought comes from two sources. One is an
external object or being that constantly brings to our mind a
certain thought. Its presence reminds a man of the same
thought, which he may be willing or unwilling to hold. The
other source is feeling, which holds a thought constantly before
our mind. It may be pleasure or pain. Pain lasts longer than
pleasure, for the feeling of pain is deep, whereas that of
pleasure is passing.

It is therefore that the Sufis have considered love the greatest
help to concentration, for two reasons: first, the object of love
stays constantly in the thought; next, pain being the outcome of
love, it makes the concentration stronger, as expressed in the
verse, "The bringers of joy are the children of sorrow." This
accounts for serious people being thoughtful and jolly people
being light-hearted.

This is natural concentration, which is done unintentionally.
It cannot be called mystical concentration, for a mystic is
powerful enough to hold a thought at will by the power of
feeling, whether pleasure or pain, and would not allow any
thought or feeling to work against his wishes. He turns pleasure

into pain and pain into pleasure as he may choose. To him both are the same, and both serve his purpose. Sometimes sweet is pleasant and sometimes bitter is useful, as even poison may serve as a means to heal and sweetness sometimes causes an increase in illness.

The master of concentration is he in whose command all thoughts and feelings stand in discipline. He can drill them as he likes. He becomes the commander of life and king of the world within and without.

Concentrations are of different kinds, and their difference is caused by the difference of their purpose.

There is a concentration on an object, a person, or an affair, which results in knowing all about the object of concentration. This is the concentration of a student, who receives knowledge in this way. Such concentration is looking at a flower and thinking of it with closed eyes, thinking what flower it is, what fragrance and color it has, why it has this fragrance, what its significance is, what its nature is, what its secret is.

Another concentration is the concentration of the psychic, who concentrates upon a certain object in order to exercise his mind. When the mind develops power, then he utilizes it in all things he wishes to accomplish in life.

There is the concentration of the idealist, who admires a hero of the battlefield, a king in his grandeur, a leader, a teacher, or a prophet. In so idealizing he acquires in himself by concentration the qualities of the idealized hero. A close study of history will verify this in the lives of great people, for most of them became great by idealizing, by admiring a great person and thinking of him.

Then there is the concentration of the lover. It is still stronger, because in his devotion to his beloved the lover naturally forgets himself; and the secret of all spiritual progress lies in this one thing—the forgetting of self—which a lover, a devotee, accomplishes without any special effort because he cannot help but think of the object he loves. He need not hold his mind on a certain object by force of will; on the contrary, his difficulty is to get away from the thought. A wandering mind is natural in the average person, but it is difficult to the lover. Therefore the difficulty of which the average person complains, that of keeping the mind steadily on one subject, is the simplest thing to the devotee. It is therefore that Sufis have recognized devotion as the best means of spiritual attainment, and many among them walk in the path of love.

Concentration upon a rock must naturally give the rock quality; the heart must in time become like a rock. Concentration on a flower should produce beauty in mind and body. So concentration on the brave gives bravery, on the great gives greatness, and on the holy ones gives holiness. This proves that no common object can be recommended as the best for everyone to concentrate upon, as one medicine cannot be a suitable prescription for everybody. The object of concentration must be chosen according to the purpose one wishes to accomplish in life.

When learning concentration, it is most essential to know first upon what to concentrate. One must not think, "Anything may do, as long as I exercise my mind"; one must know that the object one keeps in one's mind has a great deal to do with one's life. If in the mind there is love or at least an attachment to an individual, it may be for one's good or perhaps for one's ill; it may perhaps not be the right thing. If there is hatred for someone, it may rebound and destroy all the affairs of the one who concentrates. If there is wealth in the mind, there is no doubt that one could become wealthy, but if it worked against one's health, one's friends, or one's comfort or peace in life, what would that wealth be? If it is fame upon which one concentrates, one may have to hold with both hands an empty reputation, which might fall down at any moment, like a piece of glass.

Therefore practice of mind, or concentration, is taught by Sufis with a religious view, not as a scientific exercise. If there is anything worth concentrating upon, it can be nothing else than God. But as man cannot fully grasp the idea of God, he can only picture Him as something that can be intelligible to him. Any name or form of this world can be an eligible form to adopt as a divine form, since all forms are His. But would man not choose as such a human form with the merits that he can attach to the divine Being, and call it the ideal man or divine man? That is the *rasul*, the bearer of God's message. And yet man cannot picture any form that he has not seen in his life. Therefore he seeks a picture or an ideal to make the form of the rasul perfect so he can visualize it. But if he thought what marvel is hidden in the heart of the living man, would he deny this place that one gives to the idol made by a sculptor or to a picture painted by an artist to his teacher, before whom he is face to face and from whose lips comes the word of God, which strikes his heart and awakens the divine spirit in him?

It is at this stage, therefore, that a *mureed* (disciple) begins his concentration, called *tasawwuri murshid*. He continues it until he is so evolved that he no more needs a form for concentration; for the beauty of merit occupies his heart. When he rises above this stage, then his concentration becomes contemplation, which is beyond forms and merit. Contemplation in the name of God is held, which occupies the whole mind and culminates in that perfection which is beyond man's comprehension.

When we think of creation, natural or artificial, we find its origin in the power of concentration. God is known by His nature, so the secret of nature can be studied by observation of the secret of art. All scientific inventions and artistic productions are nothing but the outcome of concentration. So natural things, whose Creator is not seen, are also made by concentration. There is a Sanskrit saying that the whole creation is the dream of Brahma. Dream or imagination with the power of will behind it is creative, and really speaking is concentration. (This accounts for the effect of dreams and also the effect of imagination on the life of a person.)

Prayer is a concentration and fear is a concentration; and as prayer brings things that are desired by the prayerful, so fear brings things that are feared. In both cases mastery is absent. In the first case there is weakness, owing to dependence upon another; and it is still greater weakness that makes one fear.

Mastery lies in the creative concentration of mind. The mind impressed by one's faults and by one's weaknesses becomes feeble and meets failures, and it cannot hold a desired thought with hope and trust. In that case prayer alone comes to the rescue, when one thinks, "I am wicked and weak, but Thou art forgiving and almighty, my Lord. I have no power to accomplish my desire, but Thou art most powerful." In this way one can keep alive the flame of trust and hope in spite of one's faults and weaknesses.

Sometimes one can, and sometimes one cannot. One cannot when one's mind is too much impressed by one's weaknesses and faults, and when one thinks, "It is impossible that I shall be forgiven," or, "God is too far away to listen to my prayers. I, the sinner, am living in the wicked world, and God, the Holy of holies, is in heaven." Still worse is the condition of that person whose mind is impressed by his faults and weaknesses and who has no God ideal to hold onto. He is neither here nor there.

But when man arrives at the conviction that he and God are not two; that if God is the sun, his soul is the ray; that if God is the root, he is the fruit; that if God is the sea, he is its bubble, then he becomes part of nature's government. He is no more a machine, he is a man. He has a will of his own, which is not apart from the will of God. According to his self-expansion, to his self-confidence, and to his power of concentration, he accomplishes things, even such things as appear above limited human power.

CHAPTER 13

Mental Purification

As much as it is necessary to cleanse and purify the body, so necessary, or perhaps even more necessary, is it that the mind be cleansed and purified. All impurity causes diseases, as well as irregularity in the working of the physical system. The same applies to the mind. There are impurities belonging to the mind which may cause different diseases, and by cleansing the mind one helps to create health both in body and mind. By health I mean the natural condition. And what is spirituality but to be natural?

Very few think this way. So many people think that to be spiritual means to be able to work wonders, to be able to see strange things, wonderful phenomena; and very few know how simple it is, that to be spiritual means to be natural.

STILLING THE MIND

Mental purification can be done in three different ways. The first way is the stilling of the mind, because it is very often the activity of the mind which produces impurities. The stillness of the mind removes impurities from it; it is like tuning the mind to a natural pitch.

The mind can be stilled by the practice of physical repose. By sitting in a certain posture a certain effect is created. Mystics in their science know of different ways of sitting in silence, and each way has a certain significance. And it is not only an imaginary significance; it produces a definite result. I have had, both personally and through other persons, many experiences of how a certain way of sitting changes the attitude of mind. The ancient people knew this, and they found different ways for different persons to sit. There was the warrior's way, the student's way, the way of the meditative person, the way of the businessman, of the laborer, of the lawyer, of the judge, of the inventor. Imagine, how wonderful that the mystic should have found this out and have had the experience of it for thousands of years: the great effect that sitting in a certain posture has on a person, and especially on his mind.

We experience it in our everyday life, but we do not think about it. We happen to sit in a certain way and we feel restless; we happen to sit in another way and we feel peaceful. A certain position makes us feel inspired, and another way of sitting makes us feel unenergetic, without enthusiasm. By stilling the mind with the help of a certain posture one is able to purify it.

Before one can understand the use of stilling the mind, one must consider the discrepancy between advising that the mind be stilled and advising that the body not be stilled. Life is nothing but activity in all things. Inactivity of the body takes away its vigor and strength; the muscles do not have a chance to develop. The lazy, inactive person is always suffering from indigestion or some such ailment. How then can it be but that when the mind is made still it will not suffer in vigor and strength? Would not stilling the mind stupify a person? If the voice is to develop it must be used by singing exercises and by carrying out certain practices; if the muscles are to develop they must be used. How then can stilling the mind create power of mind?

There is great truth in this objection. Stilling the mind would stupefy it and render it powerless did one not understand life's secret, life's law. It is true that in life on the physical plane our exercises and activity of the day must give place to rest, comfort, and sleep during the night. If our body does not receive that rest it can never flourish. We need more rest than activity; we need more comfort than toil. If it is not given the health becomes unbalanced. As it is necessary for the body to have comfort and rest after toil, so it is equally necessary for the mind to have rest and peace after thinking and working.

Indeed the mind is composed of finer elements, whereas the body is made of grosser elements, and that makes a great difference in activity. The higher the plane of existence, the more active; the lower the plane, the less are the activities. That is why the mind is naturally more active than the body. Therefore, if after toil rest is necessary, how much more does this not apply to mind than to body? We usually take rest at will whenever circumstances allow us to, on behalf of our body. We recline on a couch or in an armchair after coming home from the office or work, and at night we rest and go to sleep. But when do we give a rest to the mind? The mind's rest is equally necessary as that of the rest of the body, and yet we always keep it in action. It is constantly at work, even if our body is resting. Even if the body is sleeping, the mind is producing dreams.

Many people stand at their work for a whole day, during which the mind is no less busy with the work on the physical planes than the body, for mind works with body. Yet they work with their minds the whole night long. The body is having rest and comfort, but not so the mind. Even in the armchair they are still imagining, still working with the mind. The mind has no leisure; it is perhaps worrying or planning or thinking over the struggles and anxieties of which life is so full. Even if the body is asleep there is still the constant working of the mind going on. There is hardly ever a time when the mind is at rest except when nature gives it rest: it becomes too exhausted to work anymore. Then the mind says, "Oh, I will have a good sleep." If it has only two hours' sleep, still one wakes up with such joy and strength that all the world seems new. If there have been dreams, one can only say, "Yes, I have been to sleep, but I do not feel rested," because that part of the being has not rested.

All this goes to show the great practical need for the mind to be at rest, to be stilled. Those who make it a principle that work is always an advisable thing are one-sided. Balance lies in perceiving that work and rest are equal needs for good health, both physical and mental.

The work of the body is sometimes kept under the control of man, but he does not keep the work of the mind under his control. This is not because he cannot do so; it is because he never thinks about it. Does one ever stop to ask oneself, "Why was I thinking? Was there any purpose in those anxious, worried thoughts?" Was it not that the mind was just allowed to go wherever it wanted? While one was sitting quietly in a chair, were not the thoughts active with things that had nothing to do with one's life, with things that did not matter in the least either to oneself or to anyone else's life? It was just a waste of energy.

The more the mind is allowed to go without purpose, the more likely it is to become a vehicle or machine, which all manner of influences around it—spiritual influences, spirit obsessions, other human beings—will employ instead of its owner. If the user of the mind is a proper person, then it may perhaps act properly; but if an improper person uses it, then the work of the mind is wasted. In any case it would not be a fulfillment of the purpose of his life. This purpose is to learn mastery, not to be a vehicle for others to use. He who does not direct his own mind lacks mastery.

All this shows that the very first lesson that the mystic learns in life is the training of the mind by concentration. It is not stilling the mind: that comes afterwards, and its benefit is even greater. If one only grasped the benefit of perfect stillness, even only of the body! We see a symbol of that stillness in the statues of Buddha or of Krishna or in the idols of the Hindus. What an effect that has! Compare it with the effect of a person who comes into your presence who is always active, rubbing his hands, moving about, raising his shoulders, making grimaces, tapping on the table, scratching, fidgeting in some way or another. Does he not make you fidget? The whole atmosphere becomes disturbed. Why? Because there is an intense activity of mind making its effect on the body. The body and mind are both in an unrestful state, which passes on to everyone who is in the place, for it produces unrest in the whole atmosphere. We may not be conscious that this is so, but unconsciously we feel disturbed.

The great comfort that one finds after waking from a deep sleep cannot be compared with anything in the world. But more than that, the mystic sees in sleep the symbol of a great mystical state. Rumi, the Sufi teacher of Persia, says, "O sleep, in thee I find the divine bliss. Thou makest patients forget their illness; thou makest kings forget for the moment that they are in a palace; thou makes prisoners forget for a moment that they are in captivity. What bliss, what joy of bliss, when the soul is freed from its limited presence, from the presence of those different aspects of life that are keeping it captive!"

Sleep is the time when the soul is free. That is why deep sleep is so great a state to the mystic. In the East they say, "When a person is asleep, do not wake him. It is a great sin to do so." Of course in the West they cannot say this, because if you do not go to your work in the morning, what then? It would be a great sin if you did not wake him!

As there is such comfort and joy and so great a secret of heavenly peace during sound sleep, so there is a greater joy, peace, and inspiration when the mind is stilled. The mind is so like water that our poets often call it the sea, the ocean. The nature of water is that as you look in it you see a face reflected there, your own image. If the water be not still, the face is not clear. When the water is still, everything reflected in it is clear.

So it is with mind. When the mind is stilled, it hears what another person says; it can think upon any subject that it sees; and when a person is developed, the mind can hear even what is said from the other side, yes, even what God says from heaven.

Therefore those the ears of whose hearts have listened to the word of God have first accomplished stillness in their lives. What an atmosphere such persons can produce, what effect their presence has. It is more than healing, more than medicine. A man with a perfectly stilled, comforted, and rested mind will at once raise up another who is going through distress, restlessness, pains, ill temper, worry, or anxiety. The very presence of one whose mind is stilled gives such hope, such inspiration, such sympathy, such power and life. All the heavenly properties run so smoothly and freely from the person whose mind is stilled that his words, his voice, his presence all react upon the minds of others; and as he stills his mind, so his very presence becomes healing.

BREATH

The second way of purifying the mind is by breathing. It is very interesting for an eastern person to see how sometimes in the West, in their inventions, people unconsciously apply the principles of the mystical realms. They have a machine which sweeps carpets while sucking up the dust. This is the same system inside out: the proper way of breathing sucks up the dust from the mind and ejects it. The scientist goes as far as to say that a person exhales carbon dioxide: the bad gases are thrown out of the body by exhaling. The mystic goes further, saying it is not only from the body, but from the mind also that impurities can be removed. If one knew how, one could remove more than one would imagine. Impurities of mind can be thrown out by the right way of breathing; that is why mystics combine breathing with posture. Posture helps the stilling of mind and breathing helps the cleansing of mind; these two go together.

It is clear even to those who do not know medical science that the whole mechanism of the body stops when the breath has departed. That means that however perfect the mechanism of the body may be, in the absence of breath the body is a corpse. In other words, what is living in the body, or what makes it living, is breath. How few of us realize this fact. We go on day after day, working, busy with everyday life, absorbed in the thoughts we have, occupied with business, pursuing motives, and yet ignoring the principle upon which the whole of life is based. If someone says, "Prayer is a very important thing," people may think, "Yes, perhaps." If one says, "Meditation is a great thing," people may say, "Yes, it is something." But when one says, "Breathing is a great secret," the reaction is, "Why, I have never thought about it."

For some years now voice producers have given great importance to breath. In reality breathing itself is voice, and the whole voice construction depends upon breathing. Then again, some physicians are beginning to see that many illnesses of the nerves, of the lungs, or of different nervous centers can often be helped by breathing. There seems to be a general awakening to the science of breath. Those who have practiced breathing in connection with physical culture or for the improvement of their particular condition, illness, or weakness have found wonderful results. This is as far as the science of breath has reached.

But when we come to the mystery of breath, that is another domain altogether. The perceptible breath, which the nostrils can feel as air drawn in and air going out, is only an effect of breathing, it is not breath. For the mystic breath is that current which carries the air out and brings it in. The air is perceptible; the current is imperceptible. It is a kind of ethereal magnetism, a finer kind of electricity, the current of which goes in and comes out, putting the air into action. This is what the mystic calls *nafs*, which means the self. Breath is the self, the very self of man. *Atman* means the soul, and in German the same word is used for soul and for breath. This shows that if there is any trace of the soul, it is to be found in breath.

According to mystics, the current of breath runs from the physical plane into the innermost plane; it runs through the body, mind, and soul, touching the innermost part of life and also coming back; it is continual, perpetually moving in and out. This gives quite a different explanation of the breath, and shows the value of something which very few people consider important. It makes one understand that the most important part of being is breath, which reaches the innermost part of life and also reaches outwards to the surface, touching the physical plane. But the direction of breath is in a dimension which the science of today does not recognize, a dimension which is recognized by mystics as being the dimension within.

Once I was lecturing in England, and among the audience was a well-known scientist. After the lecture he came to me and said, "I am very interested, but there is one thing that puzzles me. I cannot understand the word 'within.' What do you mean? Within the body? We can only understand inside the body." This shows the difficulty of reaching a common understanding between science and mysticism, but one day it will be overcome; it is only a temporary difficulty.

To give a philosophical explanation of this dimension, one can take as an example the simile of the eyes: what is it in these small eyes of ours that can accommodate a horizon of so many miles? Where is it accommodated? It is accommodated within. That is the only explanation one can give. It is a dimension which cannot be measured, but which is an accommodation.

The accommodation of the eye is not a recognized dimension, yet it is a dimension. In the same way there is a dimension of mind. One can think deeply and feel profoundly; one can be conscious of life and be more deeply conscious still; but one cannot point to this consciousness, because this dimension is abstract. If there is any word for it, it can only be called within. And through that dimension a current runs from the innermost plane to the physical plane, and there it keeps life living. That is why one can say that breath is the soul and soul is the breath. It is important to understand that one does not inhale and exhale in a straight line going in and coming out the same way, as one imagines. The real action is that of a wheel, a circle; from the nostrils it makes a circle, and the end of the circle is again in the nostrils.

The third point to understand about breath is that, just like an electric wire, it shows a glow; and as the heat and light are not confined to that wire but are around it too, in the same way the radiance of this circle of breath which goes on through the body touches every part of the body.

Another rule to be observed is that with every direction in which the current of breath goes, it causes a different action and a different result. For instance, contracting, stretching, blinking, all these actions are the play of the breath going in different directions. So it is with every natural action one does during the day. Also coughing, yawning, heaving a deep sigh, all these are different actions of breath. Besides, the ability to eat and drink and the ability to expel all that one has in the body are results of different directions through which breath works. And if the breath does not work in one direction, then that particular activity of the body is stopped. This is a science that has yet to be explored by scientists and physicians. The more it is explored the less necessity there will be for operations and many other dreadful things that doctors have to do or to give to their patients. The tendency to lung diseases, the pain of childbirth, early death, all these will be avoided when the science of breath is well understood by the scientists of the day and practiced by the generality.

The picture of God and souls is that of the sun and its rays. The rays are not different from the sun; the sun is not different from the rays; yet there is one sun and many rays. The rays have no existence of their own; they are only an action of the sun. They are not separate from the sun, and yet they appear to be many different rays. The one sun gives the idea of one center. So it is with God and man. What is God? The spirit which projects different rays; and each ray is a soul. Therefore the breath is that current which is a ray, a ray which comes from that sun which is the spirit of God. This ray is the sign of life. What is the body? The body is only a cover over the ray. When the ray has withdrawn itself from this cover, the body becomes a corpse.

Then there is another cover, which is the mind. The difference between mind and heart is like that between the surface and the bottom. It is the surface of the heart which is mind, and it is the depth of the mind which is heart. The mind expresses the faculty of thinking; the heart of feeling. There is an inner garb, a garb worn by the same thing, which is called breath. Therefore, if the ray which is the breath has withdrawn itself from the body, it still exists, for it has another garb within. The outer garb was the body; the inner garb is the mind. The breath continues to exist: if it is lost in that garb which is called mind, then it has another garb, finer still, called the soul. Breath runs through all three, body, mind, and soul.

From this point of view one will realize that man has never been separated from God; that with every breath man touches God. He is linked with God by the current of breath just as people draw water from a well, the rope in their hands and the jug of water in the well. The jug holds the water, but the rope is in the hand. Insofar as our soul is in the spirit of God, it is the ray of the divine sun, while the other end of it is what we call breath. We only see it reaching so far and no further, because it is only the higher part of the physical body that touches different planes. The breath goes there, but we do not see its action. The action of breath in our body is limited, but in reality this current, this breath, connects the body with the divine spirit, connecting God and man in one current.

The central current of our mind is also breath. That is why we do not only breathe through the body, but also through the mind, and through the soul too. Furthermore, death is only the departing of the body from this main current which we call breath. But when the body has departed the mind still adheres to it; and if the mind is living, the person is living also. This is what gives us proof of the hereafter. Many will say, "How uninteresting to live after death not as an individual, a body, but as a mind!" But it is the mind which has made the body; the mind is more self-sufficient than we can imagine. The mind is in a sphere in which it has its own body, just as this physical body belongs to the physical sphere. The body of the mind is as sufficient and even more concrete than the body we have in the physical world, for the reason that the physical body is very limited and is subject to death and decay. The body of the mind, which is ethereal, lasts long, being less dependent upon food and water; it is maintained more by breath than by anything else. We are maintained even in this physical world chiefly by breath, although we recognize bread and water and other food as our sustenance. If we only knew that bread and water are not even a hundredth part of our sustenance compared with what breath does in our life! We can be without food for some days, but we cannot exist five minutes without breath.

Since breath has such great importance, the greatest possible importance, it is clear that the way to bring order and harmony to our body, to bring order and harmony to our mind, to harmonize mind with body, and to harmonize body and mind with soul, is by the breath. It is the development of breath, the knowledge of breath, the practice of breath which help us to get ourselves straightened out, to put ourselves in tune, to bring order into our being. There are many who without proper guidance and knowledge practice breath. Year after year they go on, and very little result is achieved. Many go out of their minds, and very often the little veins of the brain and chest are ruptured by wrong breathing. There are many who have experienced this by not knowing how to breathe. One has to be extremely careful; one must do breathing practices rightly or not do them at all.

One cannot speak fully of all that can be accomplished with the help of breath. If there are men living in the world today who while standing on the earth witness the inner planes of existence, if there are any who really can communicate with the higher spheres, if there are any who can convince themselves of life in the hereafter and of what it will be like, it is the masters of breath, and not the students of intellectual books.

The yogis have learned very much about the secret of breath from the serpent; that is why they regard the snake as the symbol of wisdom. Shiva has a serpent around his neck as a necklace. It is the sign of mastery, of wisdom. There are cobras in the forests of tropical countries, especially in India, which sleep for six weeks. Then one day the cobra wakens, and it breathes because it is hungry; it wants to eat. Its thoughts attract food from wherever it may be, even from miles away. The breath of the cobra is so magnetic that the food is helplessly drawn; a fowl, a deer, or some other animal is drawn closer. It is so strongly drawn that it even comes down from the air and falls into its mouth. The snake makes no effort; it just breathes, it opens its mouth, and its food comes into its mouth. And then it rests again for six weeks.

The serpent, too, is so strongly built that without wings it flies and without feet it walks. Also, if there is any animal which can be called the healthiest animal of all, it is the serpent. It is never ill. Before it becomes ill it dies, yet it lives a very long time. It is said by those living in tropical countries that cobras can take revenge after as much as twelve years. If you once hit a cobra, it will always remember. That shows its memory, its mind. Music also appeals to the cobra, as it does to intelligent men. The more unintelligent the man, the less music appeals to him; music is closely related to intelligence. This shows that every sign of intelligence, of wisdom, and of power is to be seen in the cobra.

The mystics have studied the life of the cobra and they have found two wonderful things. One is that it does not waste energy. Birds fly until they are tired; animals run here and there. The cobra does not do so. It makes a hole where it lives and rests. It knows the best way of repose, a repose which it can continue as long as it wishes. (We cannot do this. Of all creatures, we human beings know least about repose. We only know about work, not about repose. We attach every importance to work, but none to rest; this is because we do not find anything in rest, but everything in work. The work of rest we do not see.)

The natural breathing capacity of the cobra is such as no other creature shows. That capacity goes as a straight line throughout its body. The current which it gets from space and which runs through it gives it lightness, energy, radiance, and power. Compared with the cobra, all other creatures are awkwardly built. The skin of the cobra is so very soft and of such silky texture, and in a moment's time it can shed its skin and be new, just as if born anew. The mystics have learned from it. They say, "We must go out of our body just as the cobra goes out of its skin; we must go out of our thoughts, ideas, feelings, just as the cobra does its skin." They say, "We must be able to breathe as rhythmically, to control our breath as the cobra does. We must be able to repose and relax in the same way as the cobra can. Then it will be possible to attain all we desire." As Christ said,

"Seek ye first the kingdom of God . . . and all things shall be added unto you." The same things that are added to the cobra, all that it needs, could be added to man also if only he did not worry about them. As the Persian poet Sa'adi said, "My self, you worry so much over things that you need, but know that the One who works for your needs is continually working for them. Yet you worry over them because it is your disease, your passion that makes you worry all the time!"

When we look at life more keenly, we see it is the same. Our worry about things seems to be our nature, our character; we cannot help it. It becomes such a part of our nature to worry that if we had no worry we would doubt whether we were really living! Mystics, therefore, for thousands of years have practiced control of the breath, its balance, its rhythm, the expanding, lengthening, broadening, and centralizing of the breath. By this, great phenomena have been accomplished. All the Sufis in Persia, in Egypt, in India, have been great masters of breathing. There are some masters who are conscious of their spiritual realization with every breath they inhale and exhale.

If he is not lazy, there is nothing a person who really knows how to work with breath cannot accomplish; he cannot say of anything that it is impossible. It only requires work. It is not only a matter of knowing the theory, but it requires the understanding of it. That is why the adepts, the mystics, do not consider breathing only as a science or as an exercise; they consider it as the most sacred thing, as sacred as religion. And in order to accomplish this breathing a discipline is given by a teacher.

But there is a great difficulty. I have found sometimes in my travels, when I have been speaking about these things, that people come with preconceived ideas. They are willing to learn, but they do not want discipline. In the army there is discipline; in the factory, in the office there is a certain discipline; in study at the university, everywhere there is discipline; yet when it

comes to spiritual things people do not want it; they make
difficulties. They think so little of it that they do not want to
make any sacrifice, because they do not know where it leads to;
they have no belief. Besides, there are false methods taught here
and there, and people are commercializing that which is most
sacred. In that way the highest ideal is brought down to the
lowest depth. It is time that the real thing be introduced,
seriously studied, experienced, and realized by practice.

ATTITUDE

The third way of purifying the mind is by attitude, by the
right attitude towards life. That is the moral way and the royal
road to purification. A person may breathe and sit in silence a
thousand postures, but if he does not have the right attitude
towards life, he will never develop; that is the principal thing. It
is upon one's attitude that one's whole life depends; by attitude
one achieves desirable or undesirable results. Generally the
whole difficulty in the life of a person is that he is not master of
his own attitude. However learned, intelligent, or spiritual a
man may appear to be, if he has no control over his attitude and
no insight into the result of that attitude, he has not gone very
far on the path.

In Sanskrit there is a saying that when a bad time comes in
one's life, the mind changes its attitude. But he who looks at
the mind as a compass which always points in the right direction
and who continues to believe in this will always find the right
attitude. And once a person has a key to his attitude in life,
then everything can be of use to him, as for instance humility
and pride. The one who has humility as his principle is
incapable of pride, and the one who has pride as his principle is
incapable of humility: one lacks the right leg, the other the left,
and in both cases something is missing. There is a time when

humility wins, when humility raises one's position, when it melts hearts, when it is the greatest virtue in a man's life; and at such times it is a serious fault if humility is missing. But then there is a time when pride has its place, when pride has to perform a role, when it raises a person, or when it sustains him; and at that time he is lost if he practices the principle of humility. Therefore it is not the principle but making use of the principle which is the main thing.

When we tell a composer, "The music you have composed is wonderful," and he answers, "It certainly is," it is as if his whole composition has become out of tune. In such a case he would have harmonized his music by having humility. But when a person is urged very strongly by his friends to come and have a drink in a cafe, which may be all for them, but not for him, if his pride at that time helps him and he says, "I am sorry, I cannot come," that would be much better than humility or showing courtesy to them by saying, "I will come."

It is the same with optimism and pessimism. There are people who obstinately hold onto optimism, and there are others who think it is wise to be always pessimistic. Both of these make a mistake. Optimism has its place, and so has pessimism. If one looks at every sign of misfortune with pessimism, maybe one will be able to avert a coming misfortune. If for instance a young violinist, among whose audience there are perhaps fifty people who he himself feels do not appreciate him, is pessimistic in regard to that feeling, in time he will find that everyone in the audience will appreciate him. But if this pessimism develops too much, he will find in the end that everyone in the audience is against him.

There are some things about which we must be pessimistic, and others about which we must be optimistic; both are necessary in life. If someone says, "Your friend is unkind to you, he does not love you, he is not a true friend to you," and we keep an unbelieving attitude towards this criticism, it will remain negative and will have no effect either upon us or upon our friend. Whereas if we believe it, our belief in time will allow the same attribute to manifest in our friend. When a man says, "I am going to fight, but I doubt if we shall win," he had better not fight. But the one who notices all the signs which show that there cannot be a victory and yet feels that he will succeed will surely win in the end. To have a pessimistic attitude towards all that should not happen and to have an optimistic attitude towards all that one wishes to be is a great thing. Very often a person blinded by facts falls flat because of them, and sometimes the truth is hidden by facts; but he should rather ignore the facts and keep to his optimistic point of view. The latter is like standing in space, and the former is like creeping on the ground. There is a saying in India, which everyone there knows, "If the attitude is right, then all will become easy"; and by right attitude is meant the proper attitude towards life.

Then there is the question of hopefulness and resignation. Resignation is the attribute of the saints, and hopefulness is the attribute of the masters, but in all the illuminated souls there is a balance. The preferable resignation is resignation to the past. We should be resigned to all that we have suffered, to all the pain we have gone through, to all that has gone wrong, to all that we have lost; but we should not continue that resignation for the things of the present, because the present should be met with hopefulness. By being hopeful one is sometimes able to change one's life, while by being resigned one allows conditions to continue throughout life.

Even such a great and wonderful attribute as contentment, which is the sign of the saints, can sometimes prove to be disadvantageous in one's life. When a person is contented with his life's conditions, this will affect his enthusiasm, and in time it will become paralyzed; whereas his discontented heart emits an enthusiasm which becomes a battery enabling him to go forward. Very often contentment proves a fault in people who may show harmony, calmness, peace, and kindness in their nature, but who at the same time do not go forward. But with things that cannot be helped, situations that cannot be changed, conditions that will always remain the same, one may just as well be contented. Besides, if one has risen above certain things in life one does not attach any more importance to them; to be contented in that case is the contentment of the sages, of the wise. However, if one wishes to obtain things which one considers to be of great importance to one, one should not practice contentment but enthusiasm. One should let enthusiasm grow so that the will power may use that enthusiasm to produce the desired results from it.

The right attitude is to keep a balance between reason and hopefulness. There must be facts, and there must be will together with the facts. Hopefulness should be built upon a ground which is solid and strong. If a person has a hopeful attitude firmly built upon the ground of reason, he will no doubt achieve success.

But the question is, what is the right attitude? The right attitude depends on how favorably one regards one's own shortcomings. Very often one is ready to defend oneself for one's faults and errors, one is willing to make one's wrong right. But one has not that attitude towards others. One takes them to task when it comes to judging them. It is so easy to disapprove of others! It is so easy to take a step further still and to hate others. When one is acting in this manner, one does not think one does any wrong. Although it is a condition which develops within, one only sees it without; all the badness which accumulates within oneself, one sees in another person. Therefore man is always in an illusion; he is always pleased with himself and always blaming others. And the extraordinary thing is that it is the most blameworthy who blames most. But it is expressed better the other way round: because one blames most, one becomes most blameworthy.

There is beauty of form, of color, of line, of manner, of character. In some persons beauty is lacking; in other persons there is more of it. It is only the comparison that makes us think that one person is better than the other. If we did not compare, then every person would be good; the comparison makes us consider one thing more beautiful than another. But if we looked more carefully we would see the beauty that is in that other one too. Very often our comparison is not right for the reason that although today we determine in our mind what is good and beautiful, we are liable to change that conception in a month's or a year's time. That shows us that when we look at something we are capable of appreciating it only if its beauty manifests to our view.

There is nothing to be surprised at when one person arrives at the stage where he says, "Everything I see in this world, I love it all in spite of all pains and struggles and difficulties; it is all worthwhile," while another says, "It is all miserable; life is ugly; there is no speck of beauty in this world." Each is right from his point of view; they are both sincere. But they differ because they look at it differently. Each of these persons has his reason to approve of life or to disapprove of it. Only, the one benefits himself by the vision of beauty, and the other loses by not appreciating, by not seeing the beauty.

By a wrong attitude, therefore, a person accumulates in his mind undesirable impressions coming from people, since no one in this world is perfect. Everyone has a side which can be criticized and wants repairing. When one looks at that side, one accumulates impressions which make one more and more imperfect because they collect imperfection, and then that becomes one's world. And when the mind has become a sponge full of undesirable impressions, then what is emitted from it is undesirable also. No one can speak ill of another without making the illness his own, because the one speaking ill of others is ill himself.

Thus the purification of the mind, from a moral point of view, should be learned in one's everyday life by trying to consider things sympathetically, favorably, by looking at others as one looks at oneself, by putting oneself in their position instead of accusing others on seeing their infirmities. Souls on earth are born imperfect and show imperfection, and from this they develop naturally, coming to perfection. If all were perfect, there would have been no purpose in their creation. And manifestation has taken place so that every being here may rise from imperfection towards perfection. That is the object and joy of life, and for that this world was created. And if we expected every person to be perfect and conditions to be perfect, then there would be no joy in living and no purpose in coming here.

Purification of the mind therefore means to rid it of all undesirable impressions; not only of the shortcomings of others, but one must arrive at that stage where one forgets one's own shortcomings. I have seen righteous people who have accused themselves of their errors until they became error themselves. Concentrating all the time on error means engraving the error upon the mind. The best principle is to forget others and to forget ourselves, and to set our minds upon accumulating all that is good and beautiful.

There is a very significant occupation among the street boys in India. They take the earth from a certain place, and they have a way of finding in that earth some metal such as gold or silver. All day long their hands are in the dust, but looking for what? Looking for gold and silver.

When in this world of imperfection we seek for all that is good and beautiful, there are many chances of disappointment. But at the same time if we keep on looking for it—not looking at the dust but looking for the gold—we shall find it. And once we begin to find it we shall find more and more. There comes a time in the life of a man when he can see some good in the worst man in the world. And when he has reached that point, though the good were covered with a thousand covers, he would put his hand on what is good, because he looks for good and attracts what is good.

CHAPTER 14

Unlearning

What does learning mean? Learning means fixing ideas and making them material. When an idea is fixed in mind, it becomes tangible, and that knowledge becomes a kind of veil for any other knowledge that can illuminate the path through life. Unlearning is a process by which one rises above what one has learned. What one learns in life is most useful after one has attained spiritual realization, in order to express it, but it can only be a hindrance in progress in the spiritual path unless one knows how to unlearn.

How does one unlearn? Does one forget things? It is not necessary to forget in order to unlearn. Unlearning is looking at things from an opposite point of view, seeing things from another angle as clearly as one is able to see from the angle from which one is used to looking at them. It is this experience that leads one to perfection. The knowledge that keeps man narrow is the knowledge which is not unlearned, but once one has unlearned, one sees everything in life from two opposite angles, and that gives one a great mastery. It is just like looking from both eyes, to make a thing complete.

It is most difficult to forget what one has once learned, but the process of spiritual attainment is through unlearning. People consider their belief to be their religion, but in reality belief is a steppingstone to religion. If I were to picture belief, I would say that it is just like a staircase that leads on to higher realization. But instead of going up the staircase, people stand on it. It is just like running water that does not flow anymore. People have made their belief rigid, and therefore instead of being benefited by it they are going backwards. If it were not so, all the believers in God, in truth, and in the hereafter would be better than the unbelievers, but what happens is that they are worse, because they have nailed their own feet to their belief.

Very often I am in a position where I can say very little, especially when a person comes to me with his preconceived ideas and wants to take my guidance on the spiritual path, yet his first intention is to see if his thoughts fit in with mine and if my thoughts fit in with his. He cannot make himself empty for the direction given. He has not come to follow my thoughts, but to confirm to himself that his idea is right. Among a hundred persons who come for spiritual guidance, ninety come out of that tap. What does it show? That they do not want to give up their own ideas, they want to have them confirmed.

Spiritual attainment from beginning to end is unlearning what one has learned. What one has learned is in oneself. How does one unlearn? One can do it by becoming wiser. The more wise one becomes, the more one is able to contradict one's own ideas; the less wisdom one has, the more one holds onto one's ideas. In the wisest person there is willingness to submit to others, and the most foolish person is always ready to stand firm to support his own ideas. The reason is that the wise person can easily give up his thought, while the foolish one holds onto it. That is why he does not progress.

Mental purification therefore is the only method by which one can reach the spiritual goal. In order to accomplish this one has to look at another person's point of view, for in reality every point of view is one's own point of view. The vaster one becomes, the greater the realization that comes to one, the more one sees that every point of view is all right. If one is able to expand oneself to the consciousness of another person, one's consciousness becomes as large as two persons'. And so it can be as large as a thousand persons' when one accustoms oneself to try and see what others think.

The next step in mental purification is to be able to see the right of the wrong and the wrong of the right, and the evil of the good and the good of the evil. It is a difficult task, but once one has accomplished this, one rises above good and evil.

One must be able to see the pain in pleasure and the pleasure in pain; the gain in loss and the loss in gain. What generally happens is that one is blunted to one thing and one's eyes are open to another thing; that one does not see the loss or that one does not see the gain; that if one recognizes the right, one does not recognize the wrong.

Mental purification means that impressions such as good and bad, wrong and right, gain and loss, pleasure and pain, these opposites which block the mind must be cleared out. Then one can see the enemy in the friend and the friend in the enemy. When one can recognize poison in nectar and nectar in poison, that is the time when death and life become one too. Opposites no more remain opposites before one. That is mental purification, and those who come to this stage are the living sages.

The third step in mental purification is to identify oneself with what one is not. By this one purifies one's mind from impressions of one's own false identity. I will give as an example the story of a sage in India. The youth asked his mother, who was a peasant woman living in a village, "What is the best occupation, Mother?" And the mother said, "I do not know, Son, except that those who searched after the highest in life went in search of God." "Then where must I go, Mother?" he asked. She answered, "I do not know whether it is practical or not, but they say in solitude, in the forest."

So he went there and for a long time lived a life of patience and solitude. And once or twice in between he came to see his mother. Sometimes his patience was exhausted, his heart broken. Sometimes he was disappointed in not finding God. And each time the mother sent him back with stronger advice. At the third visit he said, "Now I have been there a long time." "Yes," said his mother, "now I think you are ready to go to a teacher." So he went to see a teacher.

There were many pupils learning under that teacher. Every pupil had a little room to himself for meditation, and this pupil also was told to go into a certain room to meditate. The teacher asked, "Is there anything you love in the world?" This young man, having been away from home since childhood, having not seen anything of the world, could think of no one he knew except of the little cow that was in his house. He said, "I love the cow in our house." The teacher said, "Then think of the cow in your meditation."

All the other pupils came and went, and sat in their rooms for fifteen minutes for a little meditation. Then they got tired and went away. But the young man remained sitting there from the time the teacher told him. After some time the teacher asked, "Where is he?" The other pupils answered, "We don't know. He must be in his room." They went to look for him; the door was closed and there was no answer.

The teacher went himself and opened the door, and there he saw the pupil sitting in meditation, fully absorbed in it. And when the teacher called him by name, he answered in the sound of the cow. The teacher said, "Come out." He answered, "My horns are too large to pass through the door."

Then the teacher said to his pupils, "Look, this is the living example of meditation. You are meditating on God and you do

not know where God is, but he is meditating on the cow and he
has become the cow. He has lost his identity; he has identified
himself with the object on which he meditates.

All the difficulty in our life is that we cannot come out of a
false conception. I will give another example. Once I was trying
to help a person who was ill, who had had rheumatism for
twenty years. This woman was in bed; she could not move her
joints. I came to her and told her, "Now do this, and I will
come again in two weeks' time." When I came two weeks later,
she had already begun to move her joints. And I said, "In six
weeks I will come back." In six weeks she got up from bed and
had still greater hope of being cured.

Nevertheless, her patience was not so great as it ought to have
been. One day she was lying in bed and thought, "Can I ever
be cured?" The moment she had that thought she went back to
the same condition, because her soul had identified itself with a
sick person. For her to see her own well-being was impossible;
she could not imagine that she would ever be quite well. She
could not believe her eyes that her joints were moving.

People can be well in their bodies but not in their minds.
Very often they hold onto an illness which they could get rid of.
And the same thing happens with misery. People who are
conscious of misery attract miseries. They are their own misery.
It is not that misfortune is interested in them, but that they are
interested in misfortune. Misfortune does not choose people;
people choose misfortune. They hold the thought of it, and that
thought becomes their own. When a person is convinced that he
is going downward, he goes downward; his thought is helping
him to sink.

The Sufis have their own way of teaching purification
through identification with something else: very often one
holds the idea of one's spiritual teacher, and with that idea one
gains the knowledge, inspiration, and power that the teacher
has. It is just like a heritage. The man who cannot concentrate

so much as to forget himself and go deep into the subject on which he concentrates will not succeed in mastering concentration.

The fourth mental purification is to free oneself from a form and to have the sense of the abstract. Everything suggests to the eye a form, everything; even so much that if the name of a person whom one has never seen is mentioned, one makes a form of him. Even such things as fairies, spirits, and angels, as soon as they are mentioned are always pictured in a certain form. This is a hindrance to attaining the presence of the formless, and therefore this mental purification is of very great importance. Its purpose is to enable one to think of an idea without form. No doubt this is only attained by great concentration and meditation, but once it is attained it is most satisfactory.

Once the mind is purified, the next step is the cultivation of the heart quality, which culminates in spiritual attainment.

CHAPTER 15

The Pure Mind

The pure mind does not create phenomena; it is a phenomenon itself.

A man who wanted a certain bracket for his room did not know where to go in the city to find it. But he had a definite idea in his mind of what it should be like, and as soon as he went out, the first shop that his eyes fell upon had that bracket in it. Perhaps throughout the whole city he could not have found another, but his mind brought him straight to the object he desired. What does this ability come from? It comes from purity of mind.

Mind can be likened to water. Even to look at a stream of water running in all its purity is the greatest joy one can have, and drinking the pure water is so too. And so it is with the mind. Contact with the pure-minded is the greatest joy, whether they speak with one or not. There emanates from them a natural purity which is not manmade but belongs to the soul and gives one the greatest pleasure and joy. There are others who have learned to speak and entertain; their manner is polish, their wit exaggeration, and their speech is artificial. What does it all amount to? If there is no purity of mind, nothing can give that exquisite joy for which every soul yearns.

There is a saying that a pure-minded person very often seems too good to live and appears to be devoid of common sense; that often the pure-minded seem not to belong to this world. This is true, but it is not the fault of the pure-minded; it is the fault of the wicked world. That world has gone from bad to worse. Anyone who shows purity of mind begins by being an outcast, and appears to be incapable of doing whatever he may attempt. But what does it matter? One can just as well be pure-minded and wise at the same time. The pure-minded can also work in worldly matters as thoroughly and as capably as the worldly man; and the one without a pure mind may be able to make a success in the world, but it will not be an everlasting success.

When we come to the question of success and failure, there is no principle upon which this is based. It is not true that one must be good and honest and pure-minded in order to make a success. Very often the opposite is more true. But at the same time one cannot say that one has to be the opposite in order to be successful. Often dishonesty and lack of purity of mind bring great failure upon one. If there be any rule pertaining to this, that rule is that the success of the one who achieves it through honesty and through goodness depends upon honesty and goodness; and the one who makes a success of something without honesty and goodness will have a failure the day he is honest and good. It is because their paths are different. The whole attitude of mind acts upon one's life's affairs; it is most wonderful to watch. The more you think about it, the more it will prove to you that success and failure absolutely depend upon the attitude of mind.

I was very interested in what a friend who was a salesman in a big firm of jewellers once told me. He used to come to me to talk philosophy. He said, "It is very strange. I have seen so often on arriving at a house where I thought they were able to pay more than the actual price of things, that I was tempted to ask a much higher price than what I knew the value to be. But every time I gave in to this temptation, I did not succeed. And again I was encouraged to do the same when I saw my fellow salesmen selling a stone to someone who took a fancy to it for a price perhaps four times its value. Why did they succeed and why do I not succeed?'' I told him, ''Your way is different; their way is different. They can succeed by dishonesty; you can succeed by honesty. If you take their path you will not succeed.''

Sometimes he who is busy developing by mental purification may have to undergo small sacrifices, minor failures. But these are only a process towards something really substantial, really worthwhile. If he is not discouraged by a little failure, he will certainly come to a stage when success will be his. Purity of mind sets free springs of inspiration which otherwise are kept closed. And it is through inspiration that one enjoys and appreciates all that is beautiful and creates all that is good for the joy and pleasure of others.

Once I visited the studio of a painter who had died. I sat there for fifteen minutes, and such depression came upon me that I asked the widow of the painter, ''What was the condition of your husband?'' She answered, ''A terrible condition. His spirit was torn to pieces.'' I said, ''That is what his pictures show.'' The effect was such that whoever saw those pictures underwent the same influence.

If we have purity of mind we create purity. In all we do—art, politics, business, music, industry—we pour out purity of mind to such an extent that even those around, strangers or friends, all have part in our joy. One says that diseases are infectious, but purity of mind is infectious too, and its effect creates purity in others. Some keep it for a long time; others keep it for a short time. It depends upon the mind.

The mind is a storehouse, a storehouse of all the knowledge that one has accumulated by studies, by experience, by impressions, through any of the five senses. In other words, every sound heard even once is registered there; every form that our eyes have seen, even a glimpse of it, is registered there. And when our heart is pure, it projects the light of the soul, just as the light is projected from a searchlight. The most wonderful phenomenon is that the light is thrown by the power of will on that particular spot in the storehouse of the mind which we are wanting to find. For instance, we saw a person once ten years ago, and he comes before us. We look at him and say, "I have seen that person before, but where?" In that moment we throw the light of our soul on the picture that was made in our mind on one occasion ten years ago. It is still there, though we had completely forgotten it. The moment we desire to see it our soul projects its light on that particular spot. The most wonderful thing is that there are perhaps a million pictures; why should the light be thrown on that particular image? That is the phenomenon, that the inner light has a great power. It is a power which is creative by nature, and therefore when it throws light, it throws it on that particular spot.

The storehouse I speak of is what is often called the subconscious mind. There are things in that storehouse, and they are alive; all thoughts and impressions are living things. There is nothing in the mind that dies. It lives, and it lives long; but when we are not conscious of it, it is in our subconscious mind.

For instance, a person was told that he must go and see his friend on such a day at a certain time. He had written it in his notebook, but then he forgot it. During his daily occupations there came a moment when he thought, "I ought to be in that place! I have not gone there. I had quite forgotten. I should have been there. Why am I not there? Why did I forget?" Now this idea that came to his memory was in his subconscious mind, and as his will wanted to know it came up. He knew without doubt that he had an engagement, that he was meant to be there, only for the time being he had forgotten.

A pupil I once had, who was very interested in spiritual exercises and metaphysical questions, left me and became a businessman. All his time was taken up with business, and he forgot me altogether. For ten years he never did his practices. One day I happened to come to the city where he lived, and he remembered his old teacher who had returned. When he heard the lecture I gave, everything which he had been taught ten years before became alive in a moment; it was only too eager to come. He said, "It is all living for me. Please tell me what to do." He was so eager to do things now. And so it is. All that is in the mind, all one never thinks about, all that one never troubles about, is there; and when one has leisure from worldly occupations, it all becomes living.

At death comes leisure; after death the mind comes to greater life, a life more real than the life here. Death is an unveiling, the removal of a cover, after which the soul will know many things, in regard to its own life and in regard to the whole world, which had hitherto been hidden. Therefore the realization of what is said about heaven and hell which we have accumulated in our mind, in the hereafter will be our own. Today our mind is in us; in the hereafter we shall be in our mind. Therefore what is mind just now, in the hereafter will be the world. If it is heaven, it will be heaven; if it is another place, it will be the other place. It is what we have made it. No one is attracted and put there. We have made it for ourselves, for our own convenience. What we have sought after we have collected. A costly dress, if it was really important, is there. If we find out that it is not important, that it is foolish, it is there just the same.

Even useless things take a form in the mind, as everything has a form. But they have a form akin to the source of the impression. For instance, not only does a painting, a picture, have a perceptible form; music is also a language. The eyes do not see it, but the ears do. So the mind accumulates even all such forms as sour, sweet, bitter, pungent, all the different tastes. We do not see them, but they are registered in the mind in a form distinguished by us; all these forms are intelligible to the mind in exactly the same way as when they come through the different senses.

Various impressions remain in the mind after death, for what is individual? Being individual is like being in a mist. When the different physical organs cannot any longer hold the spirit, then they fail, and the spirit has finished with them. The body departs; the spirit remains. The spirit is as individual as the person was individual in the physical body. After the physical body has gone, the non-physical impressions are more distinct, because the limitation of the physical body has fallen away. The physical body is a great limitation. When it has fallen away individuality becomes more distinct and more capable of working than on the physical plane.

Part Four

THE MIND OF THE SEER

CHAPTER 16

Psychic Power

The law of psychic power is like the law of all power. By power all things are accomplished: creation, maintenance, and destruction, all are the outcome of power. Of all powers psychic power is the most powerful and the most important. As success and failure can be attained by the right use of power, so by psychic power also one may meet with great success or great failure. The scope of psychic power is much greater, and therefore by it the greatest success may be gained and the greatest damage may be done in one's own life and the life of others.

The use of psychic power is allowable to those who have insight into the law of nature, but without this knowledge its use would be most harmful. By psychic power one can heal oneself and another, one can construct one's own affairs as well as the affairs of others, one can acquire riches and position; also one can destroy things.

The difficulty is this: how is one to know what is really beneficial? For man's fancies in life change at every moment, and what at one moment he thinks good and attainable, at another moment he thinks useless. At one moment he thinks a certain thing profitable, and the same thing after more reflection begins to seem disadvantageous. For instance, by psychic power a person attracts wealth, and perhaps it may become harmful to his children. Or one desired a position and occupied it by psychic power, and he has situated himself in a position where there is danger to life. By deep study of life one always sees that a gain causes the loss of a certain thing and a loss brings about a gain of a certain kind. This is the necessary thing in life; there would not be a balance if it were not so.

That which is most desirable in life is wisdom; the next most desirable thing is power. As a foolish man would not be able to make good use of his wealth, so a person with psychic power but without wisdom is apt to harm himself with his own power rather than to do any good. Every atom in this world has its peculiar charm and attraction; and mankind, so drawn by things that seem for the moment attractive—whether wealth, power, position, or a friend—does not necessarily know the outcome of their attainment. Every man is as blind in his desire of attainment as a child attracted to something beautiful, be it a toy or a knife. And when man cannot attain to what he wants he feels as disappointed as the child that is not allowed to play with the knife.

It is keen sight into life that makes man see what is really good for him. Selfish are both the wise and the foolish; only the foolish with his selfishness meets with disappointment, while the wise benefits from his selfishness. The nature of power is to cover the eyes and hide from one's sight the true nature of the things one wishes to attain. When power leads and wisdom follows, the face of wisdom is veiled, and one stumbles. But when wisdom leads and power follows, then they arrive safely at their destination.

Before practicing psychic power one must know the law of its operation and its moral. The first thing that one must consider in this way of healing is that it is not necessary that one should try to heal every disease and every patient. There is no use in employing horses when an engine can serve the purpose, and it is not wise to let men carry a load when there are donkeys to answer the need. There are ailments that a little drug or herb can cure, and to use the power of the mind for these would be nothing but waste. Therefore psychic healing is necessary especially in cases where medicine is not required or where it has no power. Diseases of the nerves particularly are mostly caused by the mind, and medicine can never cure them completely. In such cases healing is necessary. Also, in cases where one word of suggestion can impress the patient, where one word of consolation can bring the cure, where a touch of the hand can relieve the patient from pain, it is not necessary to waste time in the pursuit of medicine.

Besides healing, by psychic power objects can be gained, affairs can be accomplished, and minds can be controlled, and this is the time when we ought to be more cautious than ever. To balance life, every profit in the world has its disadvantages, and the profit of psychic power being great, its dangers are great too. There is a time when an officer, a chief, a king rules all those under him, and there is a time when the wheel goes the other way, so that those whom he ruled begin to rule him. The czar, who commanded the East and West, had to obey the cossack who was his guard. And a time comes when the psychic moral is disregarded.

Playing with psychic power is like playing with fire: your life is always in danger. He only is safe in using psychic power freely to whom the interest of another person comes first and his own after, who is unselfish and willing to sacrifice his own benefit for that of another. But one must not be afraid of developing this power and using it. It is no sin to possess wealth; it is a sin when you make bad use of it, and so it is with psychic power. You must acquire it, you must develop it, and you must utilize it as long as you are confident of yourself and sure that you will do no one harm and that you would rather benefit another person than yourself.

There are three stages of action: fancy, action, and result. Fancy is the infant stage. In this stage one hopes for a result and forms a picture in the mind. In action one is so engrossed in the effect that the action produces that one thinks little of the result, yet one has some ideas about it. But the third stage, the stage of result, shows its effects much more clearly than ever before; and often one finds one has arrived at quite a different port from the one intended at the time of sailing.

There is one ray from man's mind working toward a certain destiny, and perhaps a thousand rays or innumerable rays opposing it. How can the one ray stand against the thousand rays unless the one ray has developed a thousand rays? Even then it may fall before innumerable rays. Therefore there are a thousand things one should consider when working with psychic power. Among them two are most necessary. One begins from strength of character and culminates in the might of God. The other is wisdom to begin with; when it has developed it is insight into things and their result. It is to swim with the tides. That no one can see except he who has experienced bitterness and has gone through crucifixion in life through patience, sacrifice, renunciation, disheartenment, and disappointment, and who has learned by this the lesson of resignation and contentment with the will of the divine Being. He can see with open eyes the way the tides flow. His position in life is like that of one swimming with the tide, in which he does not help himself much but lets the tides take him in their arms. But imagine the position of one who is swimming against the tides, his two arms fighting a battle against the thousand strong arms of the sea!

It used to be thought by the orthodox that psychic power and its use were dangerous. It was considered as magic, and its practice was forbidden by the religious authorities. Saying that psychic power is undesirable is as absurd as saying that to be wealthy is undesirable, that muscular strength is undesirable, or that strength of any or every kind is undesirable. The man who looks at psychic power with contempt would seem to have no right even to call God almighty, for might in its depth is in psychic power. It is psychic power which is the proof of God's might in man.

One must know even before one possesses psychic power, and should consider after one possesses it, what manner one should adopt in using it; to what extent one has the right to use one's power on another with the thought of reason and justice. A philosopher said, "Exercise power when you have it." There is a quotation from Jilani, "My mureed, do not shrink from using power if thou hast any." With this liberty a knowledge of the outcome of the exercise of psychic power is necessary in every case. Sometimes a man's own noose catches his throat; many times a net becomes a prison to the netter; often a man knocks his own head against the wall when trying to knock the head of another.

There is no greater power than psychic power, and to play foolishly with it would be like playing with something worse than fire. Many, when trying to kill another, have killed themselves. Many, trying to separate two loving friends, have separated in the end their own body and soul. Therefore this law should be observed when using psychic power: we must send with this power such a thought that, in the event of its returning to us, it may bring a thousandfold more benefit to us than it brought to the one to whom we sent it.

THE DEVELOPMENT OF PSYCHIC POWER

Concentration is the first necessary thing in developing psychic power, because it is exercise for the mind, as for the body there are gymnastics. No psychic has ever developed his power or been able to make use of it without the development of concentration. The two great blessings in man's life are power and inspiration. Concentration brings power; meditation inspiration. The former is constructive, while the latter leads towards the ideal of annihilation, which in other words may be called absorption within. Psychic power is developed by making use of thought at will, creating in the mind the object of concentration, and retaining it, which takes a great deal of will power. It is like lifting a chair by the tip of a finger under one of its feet, and keeping it balanced at the same time, that it may not fall. Concentration is still more difficult. It is like making a pin, which has always a tendency to fall, stand on the tip of a finger. The nature of the mind is such that it creates a thought and then throws it over for another thought to take its place. This makes it difficult to concentrate upon one object steadily.

Masters of the world are those who have mastered themselves, and mastery lies in the control of the mind. If the mind becomes your obedient servant, the whole world is at your service. The king of mind is greater than the king of a nation. In order to get the mind into control, one ought to train it as one would train a horse that afterwards can be used for the purpose for which it exists.

People make concentration a part of their everyday work, but mystics make their everyday's work their concentration. When concentration is developed one may do one thing or two or ten or a hundred at one and the same time.

The one who concentrates well, his thought becomes living. When there is less power it is as a vegetable, when more it is as an animal, when more it is as man, and if still more it becomes superman. One's thought becomes one's friend, one's ship in the sea, and one's airship in the air. If we think still more deeply on this subject, we shall find that the secret of all creation, natural and artificial, is mind, which has created this all by thought.

Psychic power in plain words may be called power of mind, and power of mind in reality is power of feeling. Feeling is the spirit of thought, as speech is the spirit of action. It is therefore that concentration is the first essential for the development of psychic power. Besides that, strong feeling void of all bitterness, worries, sorrows, fears, and anxieties is necessary.

In order to express psychic power one must have strength of body. Regular breathing with rhythm and good circulation of the blood are necessary. If one does not have these, while sending power out for healing one gets the disease of the person whom one heals; when wishing to master something in life, one becomes mastered oneself; when wanting to catch someone, one becomes captive.

Sometimes in people physically weak one finds great psychic power; but it is useful neither to them nor to another, because it makes a person weaker when he is already weak in constitution. In the Hindu religion, where harmlessness is the ideal and flesh-eating is prohibited, Shiva has allowed meat for psychics, for the very reason that psychic power is power of mind and the body must be strong enough to sustain it.

Another thing that is necessary for a psychic is steadiness in his habits and tranquility of mind. It is repose of mind, in other words stillness of mind, that develops psychic power. Activity of mind lessens the power. A person who thinks more, who is always absorbed in imaginations, who worries, fears, doubts, or becomes anxious about anything loses this power. Of course the mind should not always be still, for lack of activity also destroys power; but one must be able to exercise the mind by thought and to still the mind by the will. This gives health to the mind, and thereby psychic power is developed.

The breath is the principal thing in life which absorbs the real nourishment for both body and mind. It is therefore that those who cannot breathe rightly can never be healthy; no food can nourish their body. It is always the disorder of the breath which is the hidden cause of unsoundness of mind. The breath absorbs from the atmosphere properties nourishing for both mind and body. Therefore there is no psychic who has developed his power without the development of the breath.

When the breath is developed, then only may one make use of it for every purpose. But so long as it is not developed it is advisable not to use it, for one may, instead of curing another, absorb his pains, disease, and depressions. When a person's breath is not sufficiently developed, instead of curing he would do harm to himself as well as to the other. Therefore development is necessary before the use of the breath.

THE USE OF PSYCHIC POWER

Psychic power must be used after having been collected. Therefore the desire of healing and of magnetizing should be kept aside until the power is so developed that it will overflow. That is the time to make use of it. Otherwise, instead of helping others, the psychic ruins himself.

Psychic power is like a spring of water, ample water constantly pouring. Motive forms a channel for this water and thereby limits it to a certain extent. As by the channel the water forms the farms are supplied and the water can become useful, so by motive psychic power can become useful; without a motive it is useless. As many motives, so many channels; and as many times the water is divided, so many times the power is divided. It is therefore that people with many motives have much less success, but with a single motive a sure success is achieved. Even in a motiveless person it is possible that there may be a store of psychic power, but when a person has no motive, it is no fault of psychic power if nothing is accomplished. When psychic power is directed in a channel it becomes like the sweet water of a river, for by motive several virtues are developed. When psychic power is stored up and there is no motive, it may be as wide as an ocean, but it is like brackish water. Without motive a person is indifferent in everything.

There are great souls in the East who are called *majdhub*. In the fullness of their spiritual perfection they naturally have no motive, for no motive seems to them worth caring for in life. Therefore, with ocean-like psychic power, they accomplish nothing. Those who know about their power get some benefit out of it, but they consider it dangerous to approach them. If anybody can get them to consent to his wish it is sure to be granted, for it is just like the whole ocean making waves to grant their desire; and yet from their part there is no movement. If they have said yes with the yes of another they have not meant it.

The majdhub is a marvel. In his form the secret of God is hidden, for if God ever walks on earth, he walks in the form of the majdhub.

The finest means of reflecting power is the eyes in the body, for they are radiant, and the radiance of psychic power can easily pass through them. Therefore the power of the eyes can help more in healing than anything else. As weakness is seen in the body by its unsteadiness and by the lack of control in movements which we term nervousness, it is seen most in the eyes. The eyes are strained more than the other organs of the body, for at every moment they are busy. This takes away the steadiness of the sight and the control of the glance from every man, and being a general disease, this is never considered a lack. A child in his infancy shows in the steadiness of his eyes what nature has given to man, but as he grows older he is curious and attracted by every object that invites his attention, and so activity in time takes away the steadiness of the glance. It is for this reason that many people complain about their eyes.

The mystic therefore takes great care of the eyes. In ancient times mystics, kings, and commanders used to wear a thin veil over their eyes to protect them against being strained, thereby preserving their psychic power. What difference is there when one speaks on the telephone and when one speaks in person? What is absent? The voice is not absent; it is the eyes. Words can never convey that which the eyes can. Humor, fear, strength, weakness, pleasure, displeasure, willingness, unwillingness—the eyes can express most. The steadier they are, the deeper the man is; and as much control of the glance he has, so much power he possesses. No doubt the power is of the mind, not of the eyes; and yet the eyes are the only means through which psychic power can work satisfactorily. Three things are therefore necessary: to keep the eyes clean, to keep them from straining, and to control the glance by concentration.

The psychic first drills the eyes and makes them accustomed to operating in the direction in which he desires them to work. The glance of the psychic must become, when required, like the sharp knife of the surgeon; and when required it should work as gently as a powderpuff. Until this control is gained the psychic may help some and harm some, not knowing what helped and what harmed.

The hand is the most active organ that man has; and at every inclination of doing any sort of work, he puts his hand forward to accomplish it. This shows that man's power of action is expressed through his hand. So psychic power can also be better expressed by the hand than by any other organ. The fingertips are as rays of the light which is called psychic power. Fine rays of power manifest through man's fingertips. This is the secret of shaking hands, which in reality is a psychic help to each other.

As by working with a machine a person makes his hands capable of mastering it, and as by playing the cello a person makes his fingers capable not only of playing the right notes but even of expressing his feeling, his emotion, so it is with psychic power. Every person has more or less of this power, but he can develop it by certain exercises which an initiate learns from his murshid. When the power is developed, then the fingertips throw out the psychic power that attracts and heals.

The tips of the psychic's fingers and his palms must also become the means of directing power. The whole being of the psychic becomes a magnet. The great psychics have a healing effect even in the soles of their feet. It is therefore that an eastern disciple prides himself on being even as dust under the feet of his master.

The presence is the best of all ways in which the psychic uses his power. By a keen study of life we shall notice—especially with people who are sensitive or ill—that one person when he comes into the room brings with him an atmosphere of ease, and another person when he comes adds to the pain or restlessness of the patient. One also experiences that the presence of a person may be such that it brings illness to one who is well. This proves that there is a certain power in the presence of man that heals or brings ease, sometimes without effort. The psychics develop this power.

The whole secret of this power is life. A person with life in his body, in his mind, in his soul gives life to those with whom he comes in contact; a person without it, instead of giving life, takes it. The mystic therefore by the development of power means the development of life. He absorbs life from within and without, since space is full of life, if one only knew how to draw upon it. Mystical practices, especially those with the breath, are meant to help man to absorb life which is so ample around and about him. But when man does not know this he is thirsty on the bank of a river; water is there and he does not see it.

More than drugs or herbs or any other kind of tonic, the absorption of energy from space is beneficial. Then use is made of this energy for the purpose of healing, and the person who has developed this power of presence uses no other way of healing. His presence itself is energy. He can change the atmosphere of a room in which he may be sitting or of a hall in which he may be walking; he can spread an atmosphere around and about him which can give ease to anybody in contact with him. This is the secret of the great healing power of sages.

The breath is the only power which works directly or indirectly. It works indirectly when it works through channels; it works directly when one is inhaling and exhaling. Among its channels are the physical organs of the body; all the organs radiate the power of the breath. One who knows how to direct its power can even turn water into tonic and food into medicine; he can send the healing power with a flower; he can charge any object with the electricity of his breath. The finer the substance, the more power it absorbs. For instance, bread or wine can be more charged with psychic power than stone or wood, although a powerful breath can affect anything, however fine or gross it be.

The presence of a spiritual person has a soothing and healing effect and cures a patient. The secret is that the breath which is purified and developed becomes a stream of nectar. In the first place, breath is life, and when its current is attached to the inner life, the life eternal, it becomes more radiant and it gives life to all mortals. It cures illness, because illness is caused by lack of life; it takes away depression, for it is light; when it is arisen it takes away the clouds of depression. In the East people seek the presence of a spiritual person, and often among them are those who never speak, teach, argue, or discuss. There are some who do not even utter a word of blessing, and yet their contact gives life to the lifeless, takes away depression and sorrows, clears away confusion, and heals all maladies, for it is life that they radiate, and those in contact with them are benefited. This is an evident phenomenon which needs no proof: the atmosphere that a spiritual person charges with his magnetism is the testimony of his power. People call it psychic power, and yet psychic power without spirituality is a lame power and a blind power. When the psychic becomes spiritual, or when the spiritual person develops in himself psychic power, he becomes the fountain of life continually flowing in this mortal world.

CHAPTER 17

Insight

There is no other cause of all depression and despair than the inability to see through life. Many reasons may appear to be the different causes of unhappiness, but this is the greatest reason, the reason of all reasons. Even animals in whose nature the tendency of fighting is pronounced, when they come to know one another by association, cease fighting. Many troubles in the lives of individuals and of the multitude might be avoided if keen insight were developed, for all confusion is caused by misunderstanding. Not only human beings, but all things of this world which seem of use or of no use, which seem to be easy or difficult to obtain, all are for the use of man. Therefore penetration into things is the secret of the success of science, art, philosophy, and religion, all.

It is the faculty of the soul to see, and the eyes are its instruments. The instrument does not see: the soul sees through the instrument. I have given the eyes as an example, but really the whole body is the instrument the soul uses to get the experience of life. The seeing of the soul through the ears is called hearing; its seeing through the tongue, tasting. It is the soul's knowing of the external life. Yet the soul uses different instruments to obtain different experiences.

Between the body and the soul there is another instrument which is recognized by scientists and mystics as inexplicable: the mind. It may be said that the mind is the instrument of the soul and the body is the instrument of the mind, but both mind and body are the instruments of the soul. Although these instruments give the soul knowledge of things clearly, they at the same time limit its power.

There are two aspects of sight. One is penetration and the other extension (i.e., the length and width of the range of sight). Through the eyes of the body one can see a short or a long distance, or have a wide or a narrow horizon. But by using the mind as its instrument, the soul sees through another mind in the same way as the eye sees across the length and breadth of its range of sight.

When the mind takes the body in order to experience life, it limits its experience, for the body is not sufficient; if the mind were free it would see farther. But as from childhood man has the habit of using the body as the instrument of the mind, scarcely anyone knows how to make use of the mind without the body. And as the soul has always taken the mind as its instrument, it also limits its sight and experience. If the soul could see independently of the mind and the body, it would see infinitely more.

As it is difficult to see the mind independent of the body, it is more difficult to see the soul independent of the mind. Therefore the mystic tries to make his mind independent of the body and his soul independent of the mind. For the accomplishment of this, different concentrations and practices are given. It is like effacing the external form from the mind and erasing from the soul the form of the mind. It is this experience which the Sufis call *safa* (purity from all existing things).

THE VISION OF THE SEER

As there are different qualities of sight such as long sight and short sight, so there are different qualities of mind. There are minds which can see a certain distance and no further, and others which can see a longer distance; and what is called foresight is not a supernatural, superhuman faculty, but a longer range of vision.

While an ordinary person can see the action of another, the seer can see the reason of the action also. If his sight is keener still he can see the reason of the reason. One cannot give one's sight to another; one can tell what one sees, but that is not sufficient, for in order to be sure every soul wants its own experience.

The faculty of seeing through life can be developed by observation. This is called study, and the focusing of the mind upon the object of one's study is called concentration. As by accustoming himself to lifting one thing a person can learn to lift several different heavy things, so by observing one object of study he becomes capable of observing any object in the same way. Keenness of observation is a marvel in itself. In the first place the sight penetrates, so to speak, the object one sees. In the next place, as the light of the sun has the power to open the buds, so the power of keen observation commands the objects observed to unfold themselves and to reveal their secrets.

Every object has a soul within it, which may be called its spirit. In ancient times the seers recognized the spirit of all things: the spirit of mountains, trees, stars, and planets; of rivers, lakes, pools, and seas. Penetrating objects means touching their spirit. No doubt it is easier to touch the spirit of man than to touch that of objects, for the very reason that man is more living than any other form of creation.

The person whose eyes are not steady cannot observe fully.

Similarly the mind that is not steady cannot observe well. Therefore the mystics prescribe certain postures in order to make the body stable, for mind and body react on each other, and the steadiness of the one gives steadiness to the other.

So a person who has self-mastery, who has control over his body and mind, has balance and wisdom. Wisdom comes from steadiness, and insight follows wisdom.

There are three aspects of life, and by seeing the oneness of these three, one comes to divine knowledge. To the mystic, therefore, the idea of the trinity suggests this philosophy. This idea exists in the Hindu religion, where it is known as *trimurti*. They have a religious instrument, a kind of fork with three points, as a symbol of this, the idea being that it is the three different aspects of the one life which confuse man and prevent him from realizing the one life beneath them.

The first aspect is the knower, the second is the known, and the third is knowing. In other words they may be called the seer, the seen, and the sight. They are three turnings on the same road, which hide it and divide it into three aspects. Therefore in the spiritual path this puzzle must be solved as the first thing and the last. If the barriers which divide these three aspects are removed, then the mystic realizes one life and not three.

Occult power is the faculty of knowing or seeing. Its greatest aspect is the seer; the second is that which is seen; the seeing power is the third. The reason of this is that the Seer is the source and origin of what is seen and of the seeing power. Therefore Jesus Christ called Him Father. That which is seen has in it the light inherited from the Seer. Whether flower or fruit, it has radiance in it which makes it appear. There is a verse of a Persian poet which explains this: "The nightingale has borrowed from Thee his beautiful song, and the rose has borrowed from Thee its color and fragrance."

The means that the seer takes as his instrument are the mind, which is the instrument of the soul, and the body, the instrument of the mind. Therefore the first lesson he has to learn is the relation between himself and the thing he sees. As soon as a mystic sees life from this point of view, as soon as he connects himself with the thing he sees, he can understand it much more than the average person.

Sufism is not a religion because it does not give any doctrine or principle, but it is a point of view. The ancient Vedantists adopted this view in teaching the sacred phrase *Tat tvam asi*, "As Thou art, so I am." With this point of view, when the sight becomes keen even objects become clear to the seer and speak to him. The whole life begins to unfold before him like an open book. But there is nothing so interesting for the seer to see or know as human nature, and it is he who can see and know another person.

Ordinarily there exist many barriers between one person and another, such as prejudice, hatred, reserve, remoteness, and all aspects of duality. A person considers another his greatest friend in the world if he realizes that the other understands him. There is nothing that brings two people closer together than understanding. And what is this comprehension? It is trinity with unity. Often one wonders, "Why do I not understand this person?" but does not realize that one creates oneself the barriers which separate one person from another. If these barriers are not created the soul has freedom to see, and nothing can stand in its way. Do you think the sages and saints try to see the thoughts of the other people? Not at all, that does not concern them; but the thoughts of another person manifest themselves to the saint. Why? Because there is no barrier of duality.

The idea of the mystic is to uncover himself, and this he can accomplish by contemplating on the idea of God, which is the absolute oneness. When one realizes this, all such sciences as physiognomy and phrenology begin to become like play. By these sciences one sees a part, but by the light of the soul one sees the whole.

The glance of the seer is penetrating, and in this it differs from the glance of the average man. It has three qualities. The first is that it penetrates through the body, mind, and soul. The second is that it opens, unlocks, and unfolds things; it also possesses the power of seeking and finding. The third quality characteristic of the glance of the seer is more wonderful. It is this: as it falls upon a thing, it makes that thing as it wants to make it. It is not actually creating it, but it is awakening in it a particular quality which was perhaps asleep.

This is quite natural, as we see in the ordinary course of life that by fear we create in others fearful tendencies, and when we love we create kindness. It is possible to turn a friend into an enemy by thinking he is one, and it is also possible to change an enemy into a friend by expecting him to be so. Therefore the tendency of the mystic is to turn everything into what he wishes. To turn what is ugly into beauty, or beauty into ugliness, this is what his vision can accomplish. This proves to deep thinkers that things are not what they appear, but that we make them as they are. The whole life may be made into a thing of complete ugliness, or it may be turned into a sublime vision of perfect beauty. The lord of the yogis, Shiva, is pictured with a cobra on his neck, which means that death, which frightens everyone, is accepted by him as life. Thus even death can be made into life, and it is only the difference of the point of view that makes life death.

The first characteristic of the glance of the seer, penetration, depends upon clearness of vision. The second characteristic, the uncovering of objects, depends upon the illumination of the soul. But the third, the greatest, comes from confidence in the self, called *iman*.

THE DEVELOPMENT OF INSIGHT

As there is a shadow of every form, a re-echo of every sound, and a reflection of every light, so there is a re-impression of everything one sees, hears, or perceives. But as it takes a musician's ears to sense the overtone of a sound, an artist's eyes to recognize the form from its shadow, and a keen sight to distinguish the degree of the reflection of light, so it takes the soul of a seer to see through all things in life. The seer's eye is in the heart of every soul; it is the attitude that keeps every man looking down to the earth instead of raising his eyes upwards. The average tendency is to see the surface.

It is not true that the average person cannot see any further, but he does not think that there is anything further, so he does not give himself the trouble to see it. There are many who are intelligent enough to perceive all that is behind things, but the first thing that makes their view limited is the narrow range of their interest. They are not interested enough to take trouble about things they neither know or believe. They would be glad to have intuition if it came easily. There are many who can think, but they do not wish to take the trouble of thinking.

There are two things necessary in order to perceive: one is openness; the other is effort made in that direction. When contemplating anything, the mind must be free from all that stands in the way; that is openness. One must also arrive, by the help of concentration, at focusing one's mind on a certain object. The next thing necessary is to be interested enough in all things that one comes in contact with and cares to know about that one may penetrate below the surface and find out what is hidden in them.

The most important thing in life is the opening of that clear vision which is opened by the help of insight. The effect of every emotion is to cover the insight, just as clouds cover the sun. It is therefore that most clever and qualified people often do things in a moment of passion or anger which they would not have done otherwise. The mind loses its rhythm under the strain of an emotion, and so it upsets the rhythm of body, making man perplexed and unable to see any condition or situation clearly.

It is therefore that the sages try to keep their tranquility at every cost. Life in the world brings up many things every day and hour to disturb that tranquility which is the secret of insight. Every little noise or disturbance in himself and outside can upset a person who keeps the rhythm of his whole being in the proper order. Therefore the sages have chosen solitude away from the world. But the best way of keeping one's tranquility is to keep one's rhythm under the control of one's own will. By doing this one preserves one's tranquillity in the midst of life's greatest turmoil. In terms of the Vedanta life is likened to the sea, where there is a continual rising and falling of the waves. Every man by nature seeks peace, and in peace is his only satisfaction. But often he seeks it wrongly, so instead of producing peace, he creates more struggle in life. The secret of peace is in will power. Instead of resisting the forces which jar and disturb one's life, if one would only stand firm against them, then one could attain to that tranquility which is most necessary in order to have a greater insight into life.

Man is made of atoms gathered together around the intelligence, physical atoms and mental atoms which make up his body and mind. The power which has gathered them, which controls them, and which uses them for their best purpose is the will power. When this power is absent, the body and mind both go to pieces, broken by every jarring effect coming from whatever direction. This is the reason hidden under most illness and weakness. Every mistake, failure, and disappointment in life has this reason behind it: the lack of control, the lack of steadiness and strength against the disturbing influences which come from within and without.

The great lesson which one learns, the lesson which helps most in keeping that tranquility in life which helps insight, is to be able to become like an ebb and flow at will: when ebb is needed, then to become that; when flow is needed, then to make oneself in that way; to express when it is necessary; to respond when it is necessary.

Insight may be likened to the view one obtains through a telescope. From a distance one can see a wide horizon, but when one is close to things one gets a limited horizon. In this smaller horizon things become clearer because one sees them in detail; when there is a larger horizon things are not seen in detail, but then there is a general outlook. The same law can be applied to insight. When one looks at a person one gets a glimpse of his character, and when one looks at any assembly one gets a feeling of the assembly.

The heart is the telescope of the soul, and the eyes are the telescope of the heart. Just as when one looks through spectacles it is the eyes that see, not the spectacles, so when one looks through the heart and through the eyes, what sees is the soul. The eyes have no power to see; they have only the power to help the soul to see. The moment the soul departs the eyes do not see. So even the heart is a telescope which helps one to perceive and to conceive all that one seeks; yet at the same time the heart does not see; it is the soul that sees.

It is said that there is a third eye that sees. This is true, but sometimes that third eye sees through the two eyes and then the same eyes see things more clearly than they would otherwise. By the help of the third eye, one's eyes can penetrate through the wall of physical existence and see into the minds of people, into the words of people, and even further. When one begins to see, what happens first is that everything one's eyes see has a deeper meaning, a greater significance than one knew before. Every movement, every gesture, the form, features, voice, words, expression, atmosphere, all become expressive of a person's nature and character. Not knowing this secret, many people want to study physiognomy or phrenology, handwriting or palmistry. But in comparison with the clear vision, all these different sciences are limited. They have a meaning, but at the same time when one compares them with the insight that man has, they prove to be too small. Besides, character-reading is not learned, it is discovered. It is a sense that awakens. One does not need to learn it; one knows it.

This is one kind of insight, but there is another insight, which is insight into affairs. Be it a business affair, a professional affair, a condition, a situation in life, once the insight is clear one has a grasp of the situation. For what makes things difficult in life is lack of knowledge. There may be a small problem, but when one does not know it, it becomes the heaviest and worst of all problems, because one cannot understand it. One may analyze a problem and reason it out, but without insight it will always remain puzzling. It is the development of insight that gives one a clear vision in affairs, conditions, and the problems of life.

The faculty of seeing needs direction. For instance, in order to look to the right or the left or before or behind, one must direct the eyes. This directing is the work of the will. In the twenty-four hours of the day and night it is perhaps at most for five minutes or fifteen minutes that one sees under the direction of the will; all the rest of the time one sees automatically. In other words, one's eyes are open, one's heart is subject to all that can be seen, and one catches unknowingly the different things that attract the eyes and mind. All that one sees during the day and night is not what one intended to see, but what one is compelled by the life around one to see. That is why the thinkers and sages of the

East in ancient times used to have mantles put over their heads, so that they did not see anything or anybody and could control their sight. The Sufis of ancient times used to keep their heads covered like this for many years, and in doing so they developed such powers that their one glance would penetrate rocks and mountains. This is only control of the sight. Yogis in all ages have worked not only with their minds but even with their eyes, attaining such a stability of glance that they could direct their sight to anything they wished to examine or penetrate.

Not very long ago in Hyderabad there was a mureed, rather an intellectual pupil, and he liked to talk. His teacher was interested in his intelligent inquiries, and so he encouraged him to talk, whereas it is the custom in the East for the pupil to remain silent before his teacher. One day the teacher was in a condition of exaltation, and his pupil as usual wanted to discuss and argue, which was not agreeable to the teacher at that time. He said in Persian, "*Khamush*," which means silence. And the pupil became silent; he went home and remained silent. No one heard him speak after that, no one in the house nor outside: he never spoke anywhere. Years passed by and the man still kept silent, but there came a time when his silence began to speak aloud. His silent thought would manifest; his silent wish would become granted; his silent glance would heal; his silent look would inspire. His silence became living. It was the spoken words which had kept him dead all this time. The moment his lips were closed the silence in him began to live. His presence was living. In Hyderabad people called him Shaikh Khamush, the king of silence or the silent king.

By this I wish to imply that everyone has eyes, but to make the eyes living takes a long time. For eyes see so far and no further; it is the heart connected with the eyes that can see further; and if the soul sees through them it sees further still.

An entirely different question is how to get the eyes focused. If one wishes to see the moon, one must look at the sky instead of looking at the earth; and so if one wants to seek heaven one must change the direction of looking. That is where many make a mistake. Today in the West, where there is a very large number of students eagerly engaged in looking for the truth, many among them are mistaken in this particular respect. In order to see what can be seen within, they want to look without. This is, however, a natural tendency. As a person looks without for anything he wants, he naturally looks for inner attainment also on the outside.

How can we look within, and what shall we see? In the first place, within means not only inside but also outside the body. This can be seen by a comparison with the light inside a lamp: the light is inside the globe, and it is outside the globe too. So the soul also is inside and outside, and so is the mind; it is not confined inside the body. In other words, the heart is larger than the body, and the soul is larger still. At the same time the soul is accommodated within the heart, and the heart is accommodated within the body. This is the greatest phenomenon, and is very difficult to explain in words. There are intuitive centers; and in order to see into these centers one has to turn the eyes back, turn them within. Then the same eyes which are able to see without are able to see within.

When one is able to see that way, the pain, pleasure, joy, and sorrow of every person who comes before one manifest in one's own heart; one actually sees it. One sees it even more clearly than one's eyes can see, but it is the language of the heart. The eyes do not know it.

Besides, when once the heart begins to live, another world is open for experience. For generally what one experiences in one's everyday life is only what the senses can perceive and nothing beyond it. But when once a person begins to experience the subtle feelings of the heart, he lives in another world, though he is still walking on the same earth and living under the same sun. Therefore be not surprised if you find beings who are living in another world while walking on this earth. It is as natural as anything can be for man to live in his heart instead of only on the earth. People in the East call such a being *sahib-e dil*, that is, the master mind.

And then if one goes still deeper within, one begins to live in the soul, and inspiration, intuition, vision, revelation are natural to one. The soul begins to become conscious of its own domain. This is the kingdom of which it is said in the Bible, "Seek ye first the kingdom of God." It is the soul which begins to see. And one can see still further. What enables one to attain to this stage is the way of meditation under the guidance of the right teacher.

The first thing to do is to get control of the glance. The next is to get control of the feelings. And the third is to get control of the consciousness. If these three things are attained, then one begins to look within. Looking within helps a person very much in looking without; the same power with which the heart and eyes are charged begins to manifest outwardly. The one who looks within finds when he looks without that all that is within manifests without. His sight becomes penetrating, and his influence is healing, consoling, uplifting, and soothing.

CHAPTER 18

Impression

The first step in occult progress is clearness of impression, impression of objects, people, and affairs. To impressionable minds even objects speak, so to say, of their origin, of their history, of their use, and of their secret. The impression of living beings is felt still more. A man's presence speaks of his past, present, and future. When a visitor comes to your house he brings to you either his joy or his sorrow; he brings you the effect of his good or bad deeds; he brings you the influence of his high or low mind; he tunes the vibration of the sphere of your home to his pitch; he charges the sphere with his own vibrations. If you can only perceive, he need not tell you one word about himself; you can know if he is experiencing heaven or hell. For one need not wait for heaven or hell in the hereafter, it is here also; only after death it will be more felt. Therefore the contact of a heavenly person can bring to you the air of heaven, and the contact of the other can give you the taste of the other place.

This shows that every individual is a tone, a rhythm: a tone which draws the tone of every other person to its own pitch; a rhythm which compels every other person to follow the same rhythm. That is where one feels the pull in life; that is what scares the sage from the life of the world and makes him feel inclined to run away from this world and take refuge in a forest or in a desert. Why the average person does not feel it is that, just like children absorbed in play, people in the world are pulling each other's ropes. Therefore they do not feel much; for they are pulled, but they also pull the rope of another. But the one who is tuned to an altogether different pitch from the average person's and whose rhythm in life is quite different naturally must feel the pull too much. And the only way that the sages manage to protect themselves from this is by the practice of *vairagya*, independence and indifference both in one, which cannot be learned or taught, but comes by itself. It is not lack of love, or bitterness: it is only rising above love and hate both.

How does one get impressions? All impressions reach the brain through the nerve centers. They are mostly taken in by the breath; but by this I do not mean the breath inhaled through the nostrils. He who is able to get an impression of a person need not wait to see how he will turn out; he knows instantly. Very often one may have a feeling at first sight whether someone will be one's friend or prove unfriendly.

Partly the appearance of both objects and living beings speaks, but mostly it is a disclosure of one's own spirit that unveils all things. When we trace the origin of medicine, we come to the same belief that mystics had, that all has been revealed to man. People will perhaps differ in explaining the source of all knowledge, but it is, after all, rooted in man's soul. Therefore the man who can receive impressions aright perceives the truth not only about objects and people, but even in affairs, his own and those of others. The appearance or even the thought of the affair has in it a hidden voice, telling him yes or no, right or wrong, success or failure, do it or do not do it.

But one may ask, ''If that is so, we may never do wrong; we may never meet with failures; we may never be deceived by anyone; we may never be confused about anything.'' The answer is that we lack concentration, and it is lack of stillness of mind that causes all confusion and ruin. For water disturbed never takes a clear impression; it is still water upon which the impression is clear. Clearness of impression also depends upon the purity of the water. So it is with the mind: a mind pure from all that keeps it disturbed or confused, all that accounts for impurity of mind, is the one which can take a clear impression. The plain definition of pure and impure is that every outer element that destroys the element with which it is mixed makes the original element impure. And the spirit, which is the cup of matter, becomes impure when matter sticks to it and it cannot be washed. All meditation and concentration is intended to still the activity of mind and to cleanse the spirit of all that destroys its purity.

THE MENTAL RECORD

The mind is like a talking-machine record. But as it is a living mechanism, it not only reproduces what is impressed on it, but creates as well.

Every thought which the mind creates has some connection with an idea already recorded, not exactly similar but akin to it. Thus one deeply engraved line on the mind may have several small lines shooting out from it, like branches from the trunk of a tree. The seer therefore learns to discern the more deeply engraved lines by observation of their offshoots, just as one can, by looking at a leaf, find out what tree it is from. Thus he is able to learn more from a person's thought than anybody else. As a rule every thought a person expresses has at the bottom of it a connection with some deep feeling. The reading of the deepest line is like reading the cause of the person's thought. The knowledge of the cause can give greater understanding than the knowledge of the thought only. It is just like standing on the other side of a wall. Thought is like the wall; behind it is the cause.

Often the difference between cause and effect is like that between sour and sweet. It is simple yet often confusing that the same fruit should be sour when unripe and sweet when ripe. When one begins to understand life from this point of view, the opinion one forms of thought becomes different. There is a great difference between reading a thought externally and reading it from the inside, from the source. The one who forms an opinion of the shade has not seen the reality. The effect of a thought is but a shade; the reality is the cause, the source.

What are these deep lines wherefrom offshoots come? They are the impressions which man gets in the first part of his life. In the East, considering this theory, they observe certain rules in the family concerning the expectant mother and the child, so that no undesirable impressions may touch their minds. This shows how important it is that this question be studied.

Man is principally mind rather than body; and as the mind is impressionable, man is impressionable by nature. Most often his illness, health, prosperity, failure all depend upon the impressions on his mind. They say the lines of fate and death are on the head and palm, but I would say that it is the impressions man has on his mind that decide his destiny. The lines on the head or palm are but reimpressions of those on the mind, and once a person has learned to read the lines of the mind, there is no need of the lines on the hand or face.

Can this language be learned like shorthand? No, the method is different: while every man goes forward with the thought of another, the seer goes backward. All impressions of joy, sorrow, fear, disappointment become engraved on the mind. This means that they have become man's self. In other words, man is the record of his impressions. The religion of old said that the record of man's actions will be reproduced on the last day, that angels write down all the good and ill done by each person. What we learn from this allegorical expression is that all is impressed on the mind. Although it is forgotten, it is always there, and it will one day show itself.

One can easily trace a man's past from what he says and from how he expresses it. The past is ringing in his heart like a bell. Man's heart is a talking machine record which goes on by itself; if it has finished talking, one has only to wind the machine and it goes on again. Man's present is the re-echo of his past. If he has been through suffering, even if he is better he will vibrate the same; outer conditions will not change his inner being. If he has been happy, even in a troublous time his heart will vibrate the past. People who have been against one another, if by chance they become friends, will still feel in themselves the heating of the pulse of the hostility of the past. Great kings who have been dethroned, imprisoned, still one can feel their past vibrating in their atmosphere. The past lives, and one cannot easily destroy it, however greatly one may wish to close it.

In man's speech and in his action the seer sees designs which represent the lines on his mind. A most interesting study of this subject can be made by studying the art of different ages and of different nations. Every nation has its typical lines and forms; every period shows its peculiarity of expression in its art. One finds this also in the imagery of poets and in the themes of musicians. If one studies one musician and his lifelong work, one will find that his whole work is developed with a certain line as its basis. Also, by studying the biographies of great people one finds how one thing has led to another, different but of similar kind. Therefore it is natural that a thief in time becomes a greater thief; so the righteous one after some time may become a saint.

It is not difficult to slide on the line already made on one's mind. The difficulty is to act contrary to the line which is engraved there, especially in the case when it happens to be an undesirable line. Shiva gave a special teaching on the subject, which he called *viprit karnai*, acting contrary to one's nature. He gave great importance to this method of working with oneself, for by this method in the end one arrives at mastery.

Beneath the five senses there is one principal sense which works through the others. It is through this sense that one feels deeply and distinguishes between the impressions which come from outside. Every impression and experience gained by this sense is recorded in the deep lines in the mind. The nature of these lines is to want and need the same thing that has already been recorded, according to their depth. For instance the liking for salt, sour, or pepper is an acquired taste, and the sign of this acquisition is the deep line on the mind. Each line so produced wishes to live upon its impression, and the lack of the experience is like death to that line. Unpleasant flavors, such as that of fish, vinegar, or cheese, become pleasant after the line is formed; tastes even more unpalatable than these may become excessively agreeable once the line is well engraved on the mind.

The same rule is applicable to notes of music. A certain combination of notes or a certain arrangement, when once impressed on the mind, may become very agreeable to it. The more one hears the music which has once been impressed on the mind, the more one wants to hear it. And one never becomes tired of it unless another, deeper line is formed; then the first line may be neglected and become a dead line. It is for that reason that the music that belongs to a certain people, whether evolved or unevolved, is their ideal music. Therefore it is not the music written without but the music written within the mind that has influence. This is the reason why composers resemble each other in their music, for the lines that are impressed upon their minds have been created by what they have heard; and as the first lines are inherited from other composers, there is a resemblance. In this way the music of every people forms its own character.

The same law works in poetry. One enjoys poetry from one's previous impressions. If the poetry that one reads is not in harmony with the first impressions, one will not enjoy it so much. The more one reads a certain poetry the more one enjoys it, because of the deep impression on the mind. From this we learn that not only what is desirable but also what is undesirable may become a favorite thing. Even things that one would never like to have, such as pain, illness, worry, or death, if they are deeply impressed on one's mind, one unconsciously longs to experience them again.

It is very interesting to find that if a man has formed an opinion about a certain thing or person and after a time there has been everything to disprove that opinion, he will still hold onto it because of these lines deeply impressed on his mind. How true is what the mystic says, that the true ego of man is his mind! And it is still more amusing to find that after spending his life under the influence of these deep impressions on his mind, man still boasts of what he calls his free will.

Every line which is deeply engraved on the surface of the mind may be likened to a vein through which the blood runs, keeping it alive. While the blood is running, it is productive of offshoots of that deepset line. There are moments when a kind of congestion comes in a line where the blood is not running and there are no offshoots. When the congested line is touched by an outer influence related to that line, then this sets the blood running again and offshoots arising, expressing themselves in thoughts. It is just like a waking or sleeping state of the lines.

As one note of music can be fully audible at a time, so one line of offshoots can be intelligible; and it is the warmth of interest that keeps the blood running in that particular line. There may be other lines where the blood is alive also; still, if they are not kept warm by one's interest, they become congested and thus paralyzed. And yet the blood is there, the life is there; it awaits the moment to awaken. The sorrows of the past, the fears of the past, the joys of the past, can be brought to life after ages, and can give exactly the same sensation that one experienced formerly.

The more one knows the mystery of this phenomenon, the more one learns to understand that there is a world in one's self: that in one's mind there is the source of happiness and unhappiness, the source of health and illness, the source of light and darkness; and that it can be awakened either mechanically or at will, if only one knew how to do it. Then one does not blame one's ill fortune nor complain of one's fellow man. One becomes more tolerant, more joyful, and more loving toward one's neighbor, because one knows the cause of every thought and action and sees it all as the effect of a certain cause. A physician would not revenge himself on a patient in an asylum even if the patient hit him, for he knows the cause. Psychology is the higher alchemy, and one must not study it without practicing it. Practice and study must go together; this opens the door to happiness for every soul.

EXPRESSION

There used to be courtiers in the ancient times in India who at every moment would know the state of mind and the attitude of the king, even to such an extent that very often everything was arranged as the king liked without his having uttered one word. There were nine courtiers attached to the court of Akbar, and every one of them knew the state of mind of the emperor at every moment. The seer—whose duty in the world is to live in the presence of God and who recognizes His presence in all His creatures, His personality especially in man—fulfills his duty of a courtier with every man. A person who lives as dead as a stone among his surroundings does not know whom he has pleased, whom he has displeased, who expects of him thought or consideration, who asks of him sympathy or service, who needs him in trouble or difficulty.

The work of the mystic is to be able to read the language of the mind. As the clerk in the telegraph office reads letters from the clicks, so the seer gets behind every word spoken to him and discovers what has prompted it to come out. He therefore reads the lines which are behind man's thought, speech, and action. He also understands that every kind of longing and craving in life, good or bad, has its source in deep impression. By knowing this root of the disease, he is easily able to find its cure. No impression is such that it cannot be erased.

The mystics have two processes in dealing with these lines. One process is to renew the line by putting in some other color and thus changing one impression into another. No doubt this needs great knowledge of mental chemistry. Another way that the mystic takes is to rub out the line from the surface. But often, when the line is deep, it takes the rubbing out of a great portion of the mind to destroy one line.

Naturally the mystic becomes tolerant of every sort of dealing of others with him, as he sees not only the dealing as it appears—thoughtful or thoughtless, cold or warm—but the cause which is at the back of it.

By reading the human mind a mystic gets insight into human nature and to him the life of human beings begins to appear as the working of a mechanism. He learns from this that life is give and take. One not only receives what one gives, but also one gives what one receives. In this way the mystic begins to see the balance of life. He realizes that if the gain or loss, the joy or pain of one outweighs that of another, it is for the moment. But in time it all sums up in a balance. And without balance there is no existence possible.

Every atom of man's body expresses his past, present, and future. The reason is that, in the first place, every impulse creates its vibrations and takes a particular direction of activity. This influences the heart, whence the blood is circulated through the whole body. In this way the thought is, so to speak, written on man's face.

Man's continual agitation in regard to others, his satisfaction or dissatisfaction, his love or hatred, all show in his appearance. Everyone can know them more or less, but the seer can read more correctly. It is difficult to tell definitely the marks of thought and feelings that are shown in one's appearance; nevertheless, partly by intuition and partly by experience, man reads them. There are some in whom self-control is developed, who are capable of hiding their thoughts and emotions; and yet it is impossible to feel deeply and to hide one's feelings from the eyes of others.

No doubt form and movement speak aloud of one's condition, but the expression of one's face speaks louder still. There come distinct changes at every impulse, at every change of emotion, making marks which are an open book to a seer.

The word *kashf* means opening, and it is used by the Sufis with the meaning that the human heart is as a rule closed and that the one to whom it becomes open can read it like an open book. No doubt reading a man's condition of mind from his appearance is not such a difficult thing. Even dogs and cats can know this, and sometimes they know better than man.

What gives one insight into another is, in the first place, one's sympathy. The seer first develops the quality of love. He whose heart is kindled with the love of God is capable of the love of humanity. The heart thus kindled with love becomes a lighted lantern, which throws its light on every person the seer meets. And as this light falls upon a person, all things about that person, his body, heart, and soul, become clear to him. Love is a torch that illuminates all that comes within its light, but it is the knowledge of God which is the key which opens the hearts of men.

The Form

The first thing in the study of human nature is observation of the external part of man. It has two aspects; one is the head, the other the form. This can be seen from two points of view, the analytical and the synthetic. The former is the understanding of the character of each organ and the meaning of its form, and the latter is the harmony of the different organs. A person understands half if he considers one organ only and not its combination with others.

The study of physiognomy is interesting and can help one, but one must have intuition also to help guide one if one wishes to judge. Nothing in life is so interesting as the study of human nature; and in attaining to knowledge of God, knowledge of human nature is the beginning. Therefore in occult study one must begin by studying human beings; and the first lesson is to study their form.

The prominence of particular organs or muscles shows their vitality, and the lack of prominence is the lack of energy in them. Therefore the straightness of any organ suggests straightness in nature, and a curve, where it is natural, shows subtlety of nature. A point shows sharpness of nature; roundness makes for subtlety; and the oval form shows acute intelligence. Proportion of head and body shows balance, and lack of it shows lack of balance.

Every organ represents a certain part of man's nature that may have no connection with that organ. A particular mode of standing or sitting denotes a certain nature. Crookedness where there should be straightness shows lack of straightness in nature. Organs which should be even and are not show lack of balance.

In every face and form there is always some resemblance to the lower creation, and a person with keen insight can recognize it. Intuition helps us to understand it. Sometimes in face or form, sometimes in movements, we show a sign of one or another of the lower creatures, and this signifies some resemblance to the nature of that particular creature.

The more one observes from this point of view, the clearer will the view become; and it shows the marvel of the Creator. It makes one tolerant and forgiving of everyone, by reason of understanding that none can act against his nature. Also, he who looks at this marvel begins to see the divine evidence in every face, as a person can see the painter in his painting. And it is only natural to wish to study this part of occultism in order to recognize the divine part in the creature and worship Him.

The Face

The face can explain the attitude of mind and depict the nature and character more fully than the body and its movements. Every little movement of the eyes, the movements of the lips in smiling or in laughter, the movements of the eyebrows or of the head itself explain the condition of the mind.

The ends of the eyebrows turning upwards denote egoism and shrewdness. The puckering of the lips suggests pleasure, as the twitching of the lips shows a tendency to humor or indicates pleasure. The rolling of the eyes or their restless movement suggests confusion. The movement of the eyes toward the outer corners denotes a clever brain. The puffing of the cheeks denotes joy; the drawing in, sorrow.

One can get a full conception of the character by studying the full countenance and not a part only. The study of a part always gives only a partial knowledge; complete knowledge is gained only by a study of the whole. Keen observation with the desire to understand helps a person to read the condition of man's mind, his nature and character, yet the view is often colored by the personality of the one who sees. His favor or disfavor, his liking or dislike, stands between the eyes of the one who sees and the one who is seen.

Therefore sometimes innocent people have a better understanding of a person than clever people with deceitful minds. There is a saying of Sa'adi, "O my subtle cleverness, thou often becomest my greatest deceiver."

The Expression

Man's expression is more indicative of his nature and character than his form or features. In the Qur'an it is said that man's eyes and gestures will confess what he tries to hide in his heart. Strength, weakness, power, fear, happiness, joy, uneasiness, praise or blame, love or hatred, all these are shown by the expression. The more capable one becomes of reading the expression, the more clearly one can read character.

This shows that there is a mystery that lies behind movement. There are certain vibrations that take a particular direction under certain conditions, and the visible signs of all vibrations can be seen in man's movements or the expression of his countenance. It does not take one moment for the expression to

change from pleasure to pain, from calm to horror, from love to
hate. That shows that all the atoms of man's body, the veins,
tubes, and muscles and the lines formed by their movements,
are under the control of the heart. Every change that takes place
in the heart shows on man's face, so that one who knows its
language can read it there. People who see each other often can
read such changes from the expression, because each grows
accustomed to know and recognize the changes of facial
expression in the other. But it is the development of intuition
which gives the clearness of vision by which one can see more
completely.

The eyes are the representatives of the soul at the surface, and
they speak to a person more clearly than words can speak; to one
who can read they are the signs of the plane of evolution a
person is on. A person does not need to speak to one: his eyes
tell one whether he is pleased or not, willing or unwilling,
whether he is favorably or unfavorably inclined. Love or hate,
pride or modesty, even wisdom and ignorance, all can be seen in
the eyes; everything manifests through them. The eyes can ask
and answer questions, and it is in the grade of speed and
direction of the glance that the mystery of expression lies. The
one who can trace another person's condition and character in
his eyes certainly communicates with his soul.

The Movements

Every movement one makes suggests to the seer some
meaning. A person is not always conscious of his movements,
and not every movement is made intentionally; but many
movements that man makes unconsciously and thinks nothing
of mean something to the seer. He notices them from two
points, the beginning and the end. No motion, to a seer, is
without a direction; in other words, every movement is directed

by a precedent cause. And to him no motion is without a certain result. The purpose seems to be in the cause, but in reality it is in the effect. It is born in the cause, but it is finished in the effect.

The first thing that a mystic understands by a movement that a person makes is the nature of the person, and the next thing that he understands is his affairs. The law holds here also that straightness suggests straightness and crookedness suggests crookedness, grace of movement suggests beauty and lack of grace the lack of that element. Rhythm of movement suggests balance, and lack of rhythm suggests lack of balance. The horizontal tendency suggests spread. Movement inward and outward is suggestive of within and without. Upward movement suggests wrath, revenge, conceit, or pride; downward movement, depression, helplessness, meekness. Movements towards the left and right also have their significance: the right shows struggle and power; the left art and skill.

A contracting tendency suggests fear, indifference, coldness; a stretching tendency shows desire for action, strength, power. A tendency to turn shows confusion. A tendency of pinching and pressing shows uneasiness or agony of mind. Expansion and ease of movement show joy and happiness, and stillness without stiffness is expressive of calm and peace.

The law of the tendency of the five elements to different directions* helps the seer to recognize the various elements working in man's nature. The movement can be recognized in sitting, walking, lying, and in laughter or crying.

---

*The direction of the earth element is level, and its nature is spreading. The direction of water is downward. The direction of fire is upward. The direction of air is zigzag. The direction of the ether is not particularly perceived, because it is still.

The study of these laws of movement and direction is helpful only when the intuitive faculty is developed. If the study is intellectual it is limited and rigid, and one cannot probe the depths of human nature far enough by intellectual study alone.

The Hindus believe that the creation is Brahma's dream, which means the Creator's dream. In plain words, what the Creator has thought, He has made. So, in proportion to his might, man makes what he thinks. What materializes we call happening, but what has not been materialized we do not know; and what we do not know still exists in the thought world. In the Qur'an it is said, "The organs of your body will give evidence of your action on the Last Day." Really speaking, evidence not of the action only but even of the thought is given by every atom of the body immediately. The nature of manifestation is such that there is nothing hidden except that which one cannot see, and what one cannot see is not hidden in itself, but from one's eyes.

The aim of the seer, therefore, is to see and yet not to be interested. Suppose you were climbing Mount Everest, and were interested in a certain place which you liked, wishing to admire it, or in the part which you disliked, wishing to break it. In both cases you would have allowed your feet to be chained to that place for more or less time, and by that would have lost time and opportunity. Whereas you could have gone on forever and perhaps seen and learned more than by stopping there.

Those who trouble about others' thoughts and interest themselves in others' actions most often lose their time and blunt their inner sight. Those who go farther, their moral is to overlook all they see on their way, as their mind is fixed on the goal. It is not a sin to know anybody's thought, but it is a fault, no doubt, if one professes to do so. To try to know the thought of another for one's own interest is not just or beneficial; at the same time to sit with closed eyes is not good either. The best thing is to see and to rise above; never to halt on the way. It is this attitude that, if consistently practiced, will lead man safely to his soul's desired goal.

CHAPTER 19

Intuition

Intuition rises from the depth of the human heart. It has two aspects: one is dependent upon an outer impression; the other is independent of any outer impression. The former is called impression and the latter intuition. Intuition is a fine faculty and therefore a feminine faculty, for it comes by responsiveness. Woman is more intuitive by nature than man.

Very often someone says, "This person gives me such and such an impression," but at the same time there is no reason to prove it. He is perhaps not capable of finding any reason, but nevertheless the impression is right. There are some persons—also some peoples—who are naturally intuitive. For an intuitive person it is not necessary to wait till he finds out about a person; all he needs is one moment. Instantly, as soon as his eyes fall upon someone, an impression arises which is the former kind of intuition. A person with a fine and still mind generally has intuition; someone with a gross and restless mind lacks it. Intuition is a supersense; it may be called a sixth sense. It is the essence of all senses. When a person says he sensed something, it does not mean that there were objective reasons to prove that it was so; it means that without any outer signs he sensed it.

Intuition which is independent of impression is of a still deeper nature. For this comes so that before you wish to begin a thing you know what will come of it; before the beginning of an enterprise you see its result. Intuition is sometimes a kind of inner guidance; sometimes it is a warning from within.

How does one perceive it? It is first expressed in the language of feeling; that feeling spreading within the horizon of mind shapes itself, becoming more narrative of its idea. Then mind turns it into a form; then language interprets it. Therefore it is to the feeling heart that intuition belongs.

Intuition turns into three different conditions in order to become clear enough to be distinguished: a feeling, an imagination, and a phrase. One person hears the voice of intuition even when it is in the first process of development; it is he who is more capable of perceiving intuition and who may be called intuitive. Another person distinguishes it when it expresses itself in the realm of thought. Then there is a third person who can only distinguish his intuition when it is manifested in the form of a phrase.

It is the kind person, loving, pure-hearted, of good will, who is intuitive. Intuition has nothing to do with learning. An unlettered person can be much more intuitive than one who is most qualified, for it is another domain of knowledge; it comes from quite another direction.

The impulse of an intuitive person is very often guided by intuition; the impulse of a person who lacks intuition may come from another direction, from the surface. Impulse directed by an intuition is desirable. Impulse is just like a little straw floating on the surface of the water, and this straw becomes an impulse when it is pushed by the wave which is coming from behind. Therefore a man gets credit for a right impulse; for a wrong impulse he is blamed. But if one saw what is behind the impulse, one would be slow to express one's opinion on the subject.

Very often an intuitive person makes a mistake in catching the right intuition, for the intuition comes from one side and his mind reacts from the other side, and he does not know which is which. If he takes the action of his mind for an intuition, once disappointed he loses faith in himself. So naturally he no longer gives thought to intuition, and that faculty diminishes in him more and more every day.

To catch an intuition is the most difficult thing. For in a moment's time both are working, intuition on the one hand and mind on the other. It is as if two ends of a stick whose center is placed upon another stick were to move up and down like a seesaw, and one did not notice which end rose first and which after. Therefore one needs to take very keen notice of the action of the mind, which is gained by the thorough practice of concentration. One must be able to look at one's mind just as at a slate before one; and while looking at it one must be able to shut oneself off from all other sides, fixing one's mind solely upon one's inner being. By developing concentration, by stilling the mind, one can be tuned to the pitch which is necessary to perceive intuition. If one has once been disappointed in perceiving one's intuition, one must not lose courage; one must go on following it even if it seems a continual mistake. If one continually follows it, then one will come to the right perception of it.

It is not easy to recognize an intuition. The thought waves are just like voice waves. It is quite possible for the thought of another person to float into that field of which one is conscious, and hearing it one may think it is one's intuition. Very often a person feels depressed or hilarious without any particular reason. This may be a kind of floating thought or feeling from another person which passes through his mind and being; and he, for that moment, begins to feel happy or unhappy without any reason. It happens frequently to everyone during the day that there come thoughts, feelings, and imaginings which he has never had himself or which he has no reason to have. It would not be right to call these intuition. Water which is found in a shallow pool is not the same as the water which is in the depth of the earth. Therefore the thoughts which come and go, floating on the surface, are not to be depended upon; real intuition is to be found in the depth of one's being.

The difference between imagination and intuition is sometimes puzzling. Both come in the same way. When a given imagination began to construct itself, we cannot say. The imagination came suddenly; but so also does intuition. That is why it is difficult to discriminate between them.

The truth is that if imagination is with light, then it is certainly intuition. Every imagination is intuition until it has been corrupted by reason; when intuition is corrupted by reason it becomes imagination. But every imagination and every thought with the light of intelligence open is always an intuition, and therefore to an illuminated person there is never a thought or imagination which is not an intuition; it always touches him.

The first thing one must learn is to believe in the existence of such a thing as intuition. The next is to be able to follow one's intuition, even at the cost of something valuable. Even if one is deceived for some time, one will not continually be deceived. Therefore in the end one will find oneself on the right path. But the third thing is to make one's mind one-pointed by the help of concentration, which will permit one to perceive intuition properly. Just as for hearing the ears are so made that the voice waves resound in them and become clear, so the mind should be made a kind of capacity or mold in which the intuition may become clear. The difficulty is that outwardly the work of the ears is different from the work of the eyes; but the mind does both seeing and hearing at the same time. It is perceptive as well as creative, but it cannot at the same time perceive and create, for creating is expressing and perceiving comes by receptivity.

The mind can become a receptacle for the knowledge which comes from within. If we look at people, we shall find that among a hundred there are ninety-nine who are creative by nature, but only one who is receptive enough to receive through his intuitive faculties. The difficulty with the mind is that when one wishes to receive, the mind wishes to create; when one wishes to create, then the mind wishes to receive. Therefore that wisdom which is like the essence of life and which is to be found within oneself can only be attained by first making the mind obedient; and this can be done by concentration. If a person's mind is not under control, how can he use it? It is one thing to learn, and another thing to make use of one's learning. It does not suffice to learn a song: that does not make a person into a singer. He must learn to produce his voice also. And so it is with intuitive knowledge. When a man has become qualified by studying for a long time and yet cannot use his knowledge, what is the good of it? There is a sufficient number of learned people; what we want today is people with master minds, those who see not only the outer life but also the life within, who draw inspiration not only from the outer life but also from the life within. Then they become the expression of that perfect Being which is hidden, hidden behind the life of variety.

CHAPTER 20

Inspiration

One may say from a biological point of view that the lower creatures are born with a certain instinct, such as the inclination to fly, to defend themselves with their horns, or to bite with their teeth. All the faculties they show are inborn. They are not only the heritage brought from their ancestors, they are a property of the spirit. And from the spirit all living beings get guidance in the form of inclinations. Today, as science is increasing and as materialism prevails, man is forgetting the heritage that he has from the spirit, and he attributes all knowledge and experience to the material existence of the physical world. In this way he deprives himself of those gifts which could be called his own and without which he cannot live a fuller life.

Inspiration comes to poets, writers, inventors, scientists. Where does it come from; what is its source? Why does the inspiration of a musician not come to a poet; why does a poet's inspiration not come to a musician? Why should it reach the person to whom it belongs? The reason is that there is a mind behind all minds; that there is a heart which is the source of all hearts; and that there is a spirit which collects and accumulates all the knowledge that every living being has had. No knowledge or discovery that has ever been made is lost. It all accumulates and collects in that mind as an eternal reservoir. This is what is recognized by seers as the divine mind. From this mind all vision can be drawn. The mind of the poet is naturally exalted; that is why it becomes enlightened by the divine mind. From the divine mind all that is needed manifests. It may be that a poet works without inspiration for six months on a poem, and it gives satisfaction neither to the poet nor to others, who find it mechanical. Yet there is another who receives the inspiration in a moment and puts it down. He can never correct what he has written; he can never change it: if it is changed, it is spoiled. It is something that comes in an instant and is perfect in itself. It is a piece of art, it is an example of beauty; and it comes so easily.

Inspiration is the knowledge which pours out, so to speak, from within, without any special effort on the part of the mind. But the knowledge does not come from within. It may be called within only because it is within in the presence of the physical plane; yet it is not from within, because the soul is the self within, and this knowledge is external to the soul. It is not gathered anywhere as a treasure that a spirit or angel comes and hands over to the inspired person. If it were so, then without being lettered poets would have been prophets, and without any knowledge of music composers would have written music just by inspiration.

In plain words it may be said that it is the searchlight of the soul that moves about in the spheres in which it is interested, throwing its light on the horizon in its range, watching with interest what appears, and picking up what seems good, beautiful, interesting. That is inspiration. It may be pictured as a room full of interesting things but with no lights in it. Someone comes into the room with a bull's-eye lantern and throws its light all around until the light happens to fall on the spot he was searching for, or in which he was interested. What he picks up from there is his inspiration. Therefore a poet may not have the inspiration of a musician and a painter may not have the inspiration of a philosopher, for their worlds are different. They may throw their light on all things, but they will hold it on the things in which they are interested.

Therefore the sight of the inspirational person is keen in all things; that is why he takes interest in all things. An inspired person will not be bored listening to a conversation about something quite different from his line, for he may not understand it so far as his experience goes, and yet he will have some insight into it. I remember that to my murshid no subject was quite foreign or such that it did not interest him.

Real inspiration comes from the subject of interest, and without the light within, however great an interest one may have in any study or practice, it will be with very little success. It is for this reason that among painters one comes out as successful, and among many many sculptors there is perhaps one who has mastered his art.

Inspiration is a stream, a stream of wonder and bewilderment. For the really inspired person, whatever be his work, when once he has received an inspiration he has found satisfaction, not with himself, but with what has come to him. It gives his soul such relief; for the soul was drawing from something, and that object from which it was drawing has yielded to the soul, has given it what it was asking for. Therefore inspiration may be called the soul's reward.

It is not by being anxious to receive something that one is able to receive it; it is not by straining the brain that one can write poetry; it is not by worrying for days together that one can compose a piece of music. One who does so cannot receive an inspiration. The one who receives an inspiration is quite tranquil and unconcerned about what is coming. Certainly he is desirous of receiving something; he is passionately longing to conceive it. But it is only by focusing his mind upon the divine mind that, consciously or unconsciously, man receives inspiration.

The phenomenon is so great and so wonderful that its joy is unlike any other joy in the world. It is in this joy that the inspirational genius experiences ecstasy. It is a joy which is almost indescribable; it is the upliftment of feeling that one is raised from the earth when one's mind is focused on the divine mind, for that is where inspiration comes from.

What the great musicians, poets, thinkers, philosophers, writers, and prophets have left in the world is always uplifting, although it is not every soul who comprehends their work fully and therefore can enjoy it fully. But if you can imagine their own enjoyment of what has come to them, there are no words to express it. It is in inspiration that one begins to see the sign of God; and the most materialistic genius begins to wonder about the divine spirit when once inspiration has begun.

Does it come as a finished picture? Does it come as a written letter? No, it comes to an artist as if his hand were taken by someone else, as if his eyes were closed, his heart were open. He has drawn or painted something and he does not know who painted it or drew it. It comes to a musician as if someone were playing, singing, and he were only taking it down: a complete melody, a perfect air. And after he has written it down, then it enchants his soul. To a poet it comes as if someone were dictating and he were only writing. There is no strain on his brain; there is no anxiety in receiving it.

Because of this many confuse it with spirit communication. Many inspirational people are glad to attribute the inspiration to a spirit, knowing that it does not come from them. But it is not always spirit communication. It is natural that it may come from a living being just now on earth or from someone who has passed, and yet the most perfect inspiration is always from the divine mind, and to God alone the credit is due. Even if an inspiration comes through the mind of a living person on earth or through a soul that has passed on to the other side, still it has come from God, for all knowledge and wisdom belong to God.

There are three forms in which inspiration comes to one by the mediumship of a living being: when one is in the presence of someone who is inspiring; when one is in the thoughts of someone who is inspiring; and when one's heart is in a state of perfect tranquillity and inspiration flowing through the heart of an inspirational person is coming into it. It is just like the radio: sometimes one connects it with a certain station from which one is to receive music and sometimes one does not connect it, but it remains a radio machine. If anything passing through is not received, it is not heard, but the sound is there just the same. In the same way one receives inspiration from these three different sources.

There are different processes in inspiration. It all depends upon how the heart is focused upon the divine spirit. There may be someone whose heart is focused upon the divine spirit directly; there is another to whom the spirit is too remote. His heart is focused on a center which is focused on the divine spirit; therefore he receives his message. But it all comes from the spirit just the same. It is a fault on the part of mankind to attribute it to some limited being, who is nothing but a shadow concealing God. Besides, when a person believes that an ancient Egyptian comes from the other side to inspire him, or an American Indian comes to lead him on his way, he is building a wall between himself and God. Instead of receiving directly from the source which is perfect and all-sufficient, he is picturing his limited idea. The easiest way for the genius is to make himself an empty cup, free from pride of learning or conceit of knowledge; to become as innocent as a child, who is ready to learn whatever may be taught to him. It is the soul who becomes as a child before God, longing and yearning at the same time to express music through his soul, who becomes a fountain of God. From that fountain divine inspiration rises, and it brings beauty to all those who see the fountain.

CHAPTER 21

Dream

Dream is the activity of mind which in the wakeful state is called imagination. As imagination controlled and directed by the will becomes thought, so the dream controlled and directed by the will becomes a real dream. It is true that the will loses its control and the activity of the mind its direction in the state of sleep, but if we keenly study the whole nature and its workings, we shall realize that they all are under the influence of habit. Even an infant, without knowing what time it is, desires food and wakes up at a regular time, according to the habit he has formed. Our hunger and thirst, sleep and wakeful condition, all depend upon habit.

Those who control their imagination by concentration become thoughtful, masters of their own affairs. And in the state of sleep they accomplish their purpose in the dream. But the thoughtless have unruly imaginations in their wakeful state, and in the dream their minds become like a ship on a rough sea, sometimes high up in the air, at other times low down in the depth.

The mind has a reaction upon the body, and the body has a reaction upon the mind. Therefore it is natural that a bodily disorder may throw its shadow upon the mind and produce in the mind the same disorder. Dreams of suffocation, continually coming, of drowning, of the inability to walk and speak, do not come from a condition of health. They are the results of the impressions which have been held in the mind. They are a kind of psychical disorder, a disease of mind. The mind must be cured of it. Dreams of flying have much to do with the idea of biology; also psychically they are expressive of the soul's continual effort to rise above this imprisonment of limitation which it experiences in this earthly life. Dreams of flying also signify a journey awaiting one in the future. And it is the dance of his soul that makes a person sing during sleep.

Dreams go by affinity; that is, like attracts like. If at the beginning of the night we have a sad dream, then all night sad dreams come. If at the beginning of the night we dream a joyful dream, all night pleasant dreams come. If there is one tragic dream, then all night tragedy goes on, and if there is one comic dream, then all night there is comedy. A very advanced person does not dream much, nor does a very dense person, who is quite happy and contented without troubling to think. And do not think that you seldom find such souls: you often meet with souls to whom thinking is a trouble.

When considering dreams, one finds that although it is something which is known to everybody, this subject leads to the deeper side of life because it is from dreams that one begins to realize two things. One is that something is active when the body is asleep. To the deep thinker this gives faith in the life hereafter, for it proves that when the body is not active, even then the person is active, and he seems to be no less so than in the physical body. If he finds a difference, it is a difference of time, for here he may pass from one country to another in two hours instead of doing it in a month. In no way is he hindered; the hindrance on the physical plane is far greater. He jumps from England to America in one moment. The facility of that plane is much greater. There is no difficulty in changing the condition from illness to health, from failure to success in one instant.

People say, "Yes, but it is imagination, a working of the mind." But what is mind? Mind is that in which the world is reflected; heaven and earth are accommodated in it. Is that a small thing? What is the physical body compared to the mind? Mind is a world in itself, and the physical body is like a drop in the ocean. If in a dream man is able to see himself, that shows that after what is called death he is not formless, that nothing is lost: only that freedom is gained which was lost. Death is nothing but sleep, a sleep of the body, which was a cloak. One can take it away and yet be living.

The second thing the dream teaches is that law is working, that all that seemed surprising, accidental, a sudden happening, was not sudden, no accident. It seemed accidental because it was not connected with conditions. Nothing happens which does not go through the mind, though man has turned his back on it and is open only to manifestation. In all things we see this. Every accident, pleasant or unpleasant, has a long preparation before it. First it exists in the mind, then on the physical plane.

A dream shows the depth of life; through a dream we see things. One may ask, "What is its meaning? Has every dream a meaning?" Every dream has a meaning, only the thing is this: there are those who do not know the language of the country they are in.

So it is with minds. Some minds are not yet capable of expressing themselves, so their dreams are upside down, a chaos. They see a goat with the ears of an elephant. The mind wanted to express itself but was not able to. There is a meaning in what the child says, but it has not yet learned, it has no words. So it is with dreams which are not expressed correctly. But you may say, "How can the mind learn to express itself?" It has to become itself. Often the mind is disturbed, inharmonious, restless, When a person is drunk, he wants to say yes, and he says no. So is the expression of the mind in a dream.

It is a marvelous thing to study the science of dreams. How wonderful that the dream of the poet is poetical, that of the musician harmonious. Why is this? Because his mind is trained. His mind expresses itself in the realm of art. Sometimes one marvels at the dreams one hears of, experienced by poetic souls. You will see the sequence from the first act to the last. You will see that every little action has a certain meaning. More interesting still is to see the meaning behind the symbolical dream. It is a wonderful thing that to the simple person comes a simple dream; when the person is confused, then the dream is confused. So you see a person in the dream with fear, with joy, with grief; or the dream shows sadness.

But this is not a small thing, not a pastime. It is not a dream, it is as real as life on the physical plane. Is this life not a dream? Are the eyes not closed? Man says, "Oh, it is a dream, it is nothing." But this dream can be the whole life of the past; this dream can be tomorrow. It is only on the physical plane that it is a dream. The condition into which the mind has passed makes it only a dream.

The king has forgotten his palace. Man says, "Yes, but when we awake we find a house; therefore this is reality. If we dream of a palace we find no palace." This is true and not true. The palaces which are built in that world are as much our own, much more our own. As soon as the body dies, this is left; that is always there. If we dream of pleasure, the pleasure will come. If we dream of light, of love, then all is there. It is a treasure you can depend upon; death cannot take it away. A glimpse of that idea is expressed in the Bible: "Where your treasure is, there is your heart." We can also find glimpses of this by comparing dreams with the wakeful state. Whatever we hold in our mind, the longer we have held it, the more firmly it is established. It can be more established than what we hold in our hand. Then we create a world for ourselves to live in. This is the secret of the whole life. How can words explain it?

THE TYPES OF DREAM

Let us consider now how the dreams that we dream every night are formed. Our mind is made of vibrations; call them atoms if you will. These have the property of receiving impressions, just like a photographic plate. They are continually receiving impressions, impressions of heat, of cold, of friends, of enemies. These impressions are stocked in the storehouse of the mind, so many thousands, so many millions of impressions, more than can be counted. When you are asleep and your body is resting but your mind is active, these pictures come before you just like the moving pictures on a curtain. Then, when your mind is fully exhausted, deep sleep comes.

There are some pictures that we develop very much by keeping them before us: the pictures of enemies, for instance, or of the friends of whom we often think. Some pictures are very little developed; they just come and go. That is why, in the dream, sometimes we see the faces of our friends just as they are. Sometimes we see forms that seem familiar, but we do not recognize them. Sometimes we see pictures that seem quite strange. Two or three of the pictures that are little developed join and form one picture, which seems familiar.

When you ask, "Can we dream of what we have never seen?" I will say no. All that we dream, we have seen. The djinns, who have never manifested on earth, cannot form the picture of the things of this world.

We can help the fulfillment of our dreams ourselves. If we see something bad, some misfortune, we can take it as a warning. If we see a success in some country, we should go to that country, because it was there that the success was shown. The effect is shown first in the dream because that is the first world; then it is produced here.

As to the time when the event shown will happen: the dream seen in the early part of the night will take long for its accomplishment, a year or more. The dream of the middle of the night will take a few months. The dream before sunrise will be accomplished very soon. The reason is simply this, that the effect upon the mind of the dream of the early part of the night is taken away by sleep, and its result is not accomplished so soon. The impression of midnight is fresher, and it is fulfilled sooner; and the impression of the early morning dream has nothing to take away its effect, and so it happens soonest.

There are a thousand ways of keeping away an undesirable dream, but if it is a warning, then it will be very difficult to keep it away; or, if one particular dream is kept away, another unpleasant dream will come.

The dreams that we dream every night are of three sorts. (There is a fourth sort of dream, which is a vision.)

There is *khwabi khayali*, when a person sees in the night what he has been doing in the day, when his mind is so engaged in all the thoughts, the occupations, the cares of the day, that these appear before him in the dream. This dream has not much effect upon the mind, because it is not very deep.

The second sort of dream is *khwabi ghalti*. In this one sees the opposite of the real happening. One's friend may be ill and one may see him well; but when one sees him well he may be ill. One sees someone dead and that person recovers from his illness, or one sees that someone is an enemy who in reality is a friend. When the mirror of the mind is distorted, then the image falling upon it is distorted also, just as there are some mirrors in which a thin person appears very fat, a tall person appears short, everything appears reversed. This is because of the dream's negative nature. Everything—the printer's block, the photographic plate, the humorous glass, and all things of a negative character—will show the opposite before they manifest aright. This dream generally manifests before the view of those who possess the attribute of humanity, who first think of the world and its responsibilities, together with the thought of God.

The third sort of dream is of little importance, just like the birth of a child who has died after living only a week. The same is the case with dreams produced before the view of man caused either by the unbalanced activity of mind or by disorder of the health. Such dreams have as a rule no importance, and they are surely a waste, although they create before man a moving picture.

The Mental Dream

The mind has its full play when a person is asleep, for in the wakeful state one has rein over the mind, but in sleep that rein is mostly lost. The mind is then free to produce pictures, natural or unnatural, broken or unbroken. These pictures are produced according to the life in them, and that life is given them by the mind itself. Plainly speaking, the things one thinks of often and the objects that one sees most gain life at every observation given to them. Therefore one usually sees in the dream the dearest friend or the bitterest enemy. The same thing accounts for the dairyman's dreaming of milk and the butcher's dreaming of meat. Every person's world is separate; his world is that in which he lives and of which he thinks.

The reason why mental dreams should have an effect upon the life of a person is that the line of one's fate is made on the lines of the impressions that one's mind creates before one's soul. It is therefore that an unhappy dream would bring about unhappiness and a happy dream would bring about happiness. It is not true that what is going to happen is shown to one in the dream, though one is always apt to think so. The fact is that the dream has built a bridge for one to land into trouble or happiness.

The Symbolical Dream

It is very interesting to see how knowledge of the past, present, and future is revealed to every soul in symbols. The illuminated sees the symbol and to him it is everything; to him who cannot see it is nothing. Nothing can teach us how to read the real meaning of symbols unless our own soul discloses to us their secret.

Symbolical dreams mostly concern ourselves. They show us the condition of our affairs in life and the state of those whom we love. The reason why a symbol in a dream should show us what is hidden in the past, present, and future is that the symbol is the form in which it first constructs itself; and then it changes its form on the surface. Another reason is that the past or future effect of a happening has quite a different form from that of its real occurrence. It is just as in sound there is a tone and an overtone which belong to the original note, only they are different in their effect and color.

As delicate as a person's thoughts are, so delicate is the symbol. To a simple person the symbol is simple; to a complex person the symbol is complex. One reads the symbol of the dream according to the development of one's soul, for in proportion to the soul's evolution one sees things clearly. There is no end to the interest when the secret of symbolical dreams begins to disclose itself to the dreamer. It is more than an astonishment; it is more than a wonder.

The Astral Dream

The astral dream manifests to the sight of pious beings who are at the same time balanced. It is scarcely vouchsafed to an unbalanced person, however spiritually evolved. The astral dream is the real experience of the soul dwelling in the higher spheres with the vehicle of the mind.

There are three aspects of the astral dream. One is that a person knows the real happening as it is, not in a contrary or symbolical manifestation. The actual happening manifests on the surface. The next aspect is that a person meets a living or dead friend and sees his actual condition. The third is that the astral part of the living or dead person comes and visits the dreamer.

By means of the astral dream a great many things are accomplished. Those who become masters of life control the astral plane and bring about the above-mentioned three experiences at will.

CHAPTER 22

Vision

In the vision or spiritual dream the light of the soul has fully illuminated the mind, and the mind is able to create and perceive a clear picture of the past, present, and future. One actually sees what is happening at a distance, what has happened in the past, or what is going to take place. It is like a flash. Vision may be described as the language of God which is expressed not only in words but in a picture. That which cannot be audible and that which is not intelligible when audible is produced in a visible form.

A vision is more clear in the sleeping than in the wakeful state. The reason is that when a person is asleep he lives in a world of his own, but when awake he is only partly in that world, and mostly in the outer world. Every phenomenon needs accommodation. Not only is sound audible, but the ears make it possible to hear sound. Just as the ears are the accommodation to receive sound, the mind is the accommodation to receive impressions. That is why a natural state of sleep is like a profound concentration, like a deep meditation; and that is why everything that comes as a dream has a significance.

There are two different visions, a vision which descends and a vision which ascends. The former is from God; the latter is from man. There are two aspects of the former, vision in voice and in picture. There are two aspects of the latter, the self-created vision and that which comes by response. For instance, a devotee by the fullness of his devotion may create the picture of the savior in his heart, or one who is responsive, in his full response and waiting, may attract the spirit of the savior. In both cases the benefit and blessing are the same, for it is not man who creates, even if it were creation by man. God alone is the Creator, and He creates whenever anything is created, as God and also as man.

A vision may be of anything. It may be a condition of the past, present, or future seen as if produced on a stage. It can bring an appearance of a saint, sage, or master, living or on the other side. It can show symbols which tell something about one's life in different forms and colors. It can come as sound, as words, as a song, as poetry, as a written letter, or as a fragrance.

Every unseen form that man sees in a vision, be it of a spirit, fairy, or angel, or of a teacher, sage, or saint, is according to his evolution. As highly evolved as a person is, so high is his vision. Sometimes he attracts the object of his vision, sometimes the object of the vision wishes to manifest to him, and sometimes he creates the object of his vision before him.

The goodness of the vision depends upon the greatness of the object. In an astral vision, a relation or a friend may appear to a person and tell him something about the other side of life. Before another a saint or sage may appear, who may guide him still further. To another an angel may appear, as Gabriel did to Moses, and may give him the message of God.

The traditions of the world are mostly based upon visions. The vision of Valmiki brought Rama, the great king and prophet of the Hindus. Solomon, Jamshyd, Joseph, even Abraham, the father of religions, were known and accepted as prophets by reason of their visions. The foundation of the life of Jesus Christ was the vision of the Virgin Mary. The beginning of the prophethood of Muhammad was the vision of Amina, his mother. The Qur'an contains laws and morals, and if mysticism and philosophy can be traced in it, they are in the *miraj*, the vision of the Prophet. In the Bible the most interesting part to a mystic is the Revelations, where there is a vision.

There was a poet of Persia, Firdawsi, who was asked by the king to write the history of the country. The king promised him a gold coin for every verse. Firdawsi went into solitude and wrote down the traditions of centuries. Characters, lives, deeds —he saw it all as a play, and he wrote of it in verse. When he returned to the court, the king was most impressed; he thought it wonderful. But there are always many in the world who will reject such things. The truth is accepted only by the few. At the court he was much criticized, and many showed skepticism. It went so far that they told the king that it was all Firdawsi's imagination. This hurt him terribly. He took the one who had spoken most against him and held his hand upon his head, and said to him, "Now close your eyes, and look." And what this man saw was like a moving picture and he exclaimed, "I have seen!" But the poet's heart was wounded, and he would not accept the king's gold coins.

There is no greater sign nor more wonderful proof of the inner life than vision. Such appropriate symbols and forms appear to the visionary to tell him of the past, present, and future that one can do nothing but marvel at the wisdom of the inner nature and glorify the name of God. There is a language of forms and symbols. When one does not know this visions have no meaning to one, but there cannot be made a standard of this language. Though many have written books on dreams, yet no book has been successful as to be a general standard of dreams and visions.

Every vision springs from the heart of man with as fine and delicate a form as his own personality, in as picturesque a form as his artistic capabilities, and in such metaphor or so symbolical as his poetic gift. Therefore the visions of prophets have always been interesting, for the prophets are the real poets, though poets are not necessarily prophets.

A vision is the art of nature, the poetry of nature, the beautiful dream of nature. The purer the soul, the clearer the vision becomes. It is the bowl of Jamshyd, the seven-ringed cup which is the head with seven openings. In this head the vision rises, and it shows him all whose sight is keen.

There are times when visions are symbolical, and there are times when visions are clear. They are clear at the moment when the soul is clear from all earthly shadows, and therefore heavenly pictures, so to speak, appear upon the curtain of man's heart. One may see the vision of his rasul, his savior, his lord, master, prophet, or teacher. One may see the vision of one's friends or relations, past and present. One may see faces never seen before and yet that once existed in the world. One may see djinns and angels. This vision manifests to a spiritual mind, and sometimes to anyone who may be for the moment in a clear spiritual atmosphere. No right pertains to any other person to judge the truth of the vision.

The dreams and visions that we have in life are mostly symbolical and scarcely ever plain. They are symbolical because everything in the inner plane shapes differently from the form it wears in the outer plane. The same reason accounts for the inspiration of the prophets, for many others besides them at times touch the same goal that they touched, since the consciousness of all is one. But everybody does not realize it consciously; and some who realize it do not know the language of the inner world, for the spirit speaks a language that is unintelligible to all save a few who are gifted by nature to understand the cry of truth behind it. A person who has known oranges is not necessarily able to recognize the orange tree, but he who knows the orange tree can expect oranges on seeing the tree's seedling. Sometimes buds cannot at all give an idea of what the flower is like.

Many people see symbolical dreams, and some see symbolical visions, and yet they cannot understand their effect, for they sometimes seem quite different from the effect they have. For instance, an elephant in the East is considered to be a sign of honor, but in the dream it is the sign of death. One cannot take an object as having such and such an effect in life; it is the way in which it is produced that makes one realize its result. Intelligence is a great bliss. When it is clear it helps one realize the nature of things, and by that one can read symbolical visions. The study of symbology can never suffice one's purpose, for there is no limit to the variety of nature's forms. It is intuition that helps one and makes the meaning clear.

Symbolical visions are very interesting because the forms of things and beings, their combination, and the running course with changes all tell of past, present, and future. To an intuitive person or to a seer it is an open book. Every soul has visions at very important times in its life, but there comes a time of the clearness of the soul when every dream becomes a vision, and it can increase to such an extent that a person may have twenty visions during the day.

Vision is not the only sign of spiritual progress. A person may have gone far on the spiritual path and he may not have visions. Visions are a temperament. There is a visionary type of person, imaginative, dreamy, interested in dreams and whims; and if he is spiritual, the same type produces real visions. Vision is generally vouchsafed to those whose heart can see. It mostly comes to the pious, to the innocent, to the loving; to those of tranquil mind; to those who have suffered in life, who have had patience and are tender-hearted, who are on the path of goodness.

To those who are developed spiritually vision often comes, sometimes as an answer to their question, sometimes to warn them of an unforseen danger, and sometimes to guide them toward some accomplishment in life. In spiritual development it is not necessary that one should have the above-said virtues. If one's soul can rise at will from the lower planes of existence one can dwell in the spiritual planes with mastery.

Mental vision comes to those who walk in the path of devotion and who hold an ideal in their concentration. At times when it is necessary, a warning or a guidance appears to them as a vision in the form of their ideal. Those who master *tasawwur*, the concrete production of the ideal in thought, first experience every form they see as covered with the form of their ideal. This is the first step toward progress, which in Sufi term is named *fana-fi-shaikh*. Then a vision is already created within them, and they receive advice on any point they wish for from within.

Vision generally comes when one is fast asleep, but sometimes it comes when a person is half asleep. Sometimes it comes through meditation. Sometimes when the eyes are closed it comes as a glimpse and disappears. It also comes to those who have gone through a long illness, who are perhaps abnormal in mind or weak in body. During vision the condition of the person is negative, in other words passive.

Those who talk about their vision to everybody or feel proud of it indeed abuse this spiritual gift. Then it passes away from them, and what remains with them is exaggeration and then falsehood. The wise thing is to keep one's vision secret to oneself, not to tell anybody about it except one's most trusted friend who one thinks is wise and can help on the path, or one's teacher, who knows the state of one's development.

The greatest hindrance that veils man's eyes from the

spiritual dream is the thought of self. As much as one can forget oneself, so capable does one become of witnessing the spiritual vision.

CHAPTER 23

Revelation

In the story of Moses it is said that he was looking for fire to bake bread when he happened to see a light on the top of a mountain. And so in order to take this fire he climbed the mountain, but the fire became lightning. Moses could no longer withstand that great flashing and he fell to the ground; and when he woke up he began to communicate with God.

This is allegorical. The idea is that Moses was looking for light to make it his life's sustenance, but he had to climb onto the higher planes: it was not possible to get it on the earth where he stood. Then he encountered lightning, a light which it was beyond his power to withstand, and he fell down. What is this falling down? To become nothing, to become empty. When he reached that state of emptiness, then his heart became sonorous, and he found communication with God through everything in the world. In the rock, tree, or plant, in the star, sun, or moon, in whatever he saw he found communication with his soul. And so everything revealed its nature and its secret to him.

It requires a certain amount of spiritual progress to believe that there is such a thing as revelation. Life is revealing, nature is revealing, and so is God; that is why in Persian God is called *Khuda*, which means self-revealing. All science, art, and culture known to man came originally, and still come, by revelation. In other words, a person not only learns by studying, but he also draws knowledge from humanity. A child not only inherits his father's or his ancestors' qualities, but also the qualities of his nation, of his race; so that one can say that man inherits the qualities of the entire human race. If one realized profoundly that storehouse of knowledge which exists behind the veil which covers it, one would find that one has a right to this heritage. This gives one a key to understanding the secret of life: that knowledge is not only gained from outside, but also from within. One may call the knowledge that one learns from the outer life learning, but the knowledge that one draws from within may be called revelation.

Revelation may be explained in plain words as discovery. The whole life is before us and we perceive it through our five senses, and yet there is confusion. It seems as if we see things and do not see them; we understand and yet we do not understand. It is as if we see nuts in their shells, not knowing whether they are decayed or fresh, and mostly we make mistakes. That which is living is as dead to us, and that part of life which may be called dead alone seems living.

Revelation has several grades of depth, and every stage of evolution makes a person capable of having a certain revelation. Revelation is greater than intuition, impression, or inspiration, because it is as plain as a written letter. It comes to a person who, so to speak, lives in the soul more than in the body or the mind.

When revelation comes to a person he no longer remains simply a poet, a musician, or a philosopher, but becomes only God's instrument. Then God begins to speak to him through everything, not only in melody, in verse, in color, or in light. He begins to communicate with God in all forms. Everything he sees above or below, right or left, before or behind, either heavenly or earthly, is communicative. He then begins to speak with God.

People think that one arrives in heaven after death, but heaven is really experienced from the first moment of revelation. As a matter of fact, it is revelation that makes heaven, and every stage of revelation is a heaven. So when people say heaven, it means different stages of revelation.

The first stage is cleverness; the next is wisdom. In cleverness the intelligence is in confusion, for it is active, passionately active. In wisdom the intelligence is rhythmic. When a person says, "I will not allow you to get the best of me; if you are crooked I will show you ten times more crookedness," then he is clever. But when a person says, "Yes, I understand you; you need not play that game with me; let me alone," he is wise. When a person does not know the crookedness of another and so allows him to get the best of him, he is a fool. But when he sees clearly the roguery and crookedness of another person and yet allows him to get the best, he is a holy man. He is beyond the regions of humanity; he is beginning to climb the angelic planes. He sees all things, understands all things, and tolerates all things.

Revelation is the perfection of insight. When one has revelation it means a higher development, and it begins when a person feels in tune with everybody, everything, and every condition. But in order to come to that stage one must develop accordingly. The heart must be tuned to the stage and the pitch where one feels at-one-ment with people, objects, and conditions. For instance, when one cannot bear the climate, it only means that one is not in harmony with the climate; when one cannot get on with people, that one is not in harmony with them; when one cannot get on with certain affairs, that one is not in harmony with those affairs. If conditions seem hard, it shows that one is not in harmony with them.

Revelation came to the saints and saviors of humanity. It is not just a tale when we hear that the saints spoke with trees and plants in the wilderness, that a voice from the sea rose and the saints heard it, that masters talked with the sun, moon, and stars. For the deeper a person dives into life, the more he is convinced that all is living, whether beings or objects, art or nature; whatever he sees, whatever he perceives through the senses, whatever he can touch, all is intelligible to him. It may not be seen and it may not be known by anybody else, but everything is communicating. Once a person begins to communicate with nature, with art, he begins to have the proof of this, for everything begins to speak. As the great poet of Persia, Sa'adi, said, "Every leaf of the tree becomes a page of the Book when once the heart is opened and it has learned to read."

When revelation begins, a man does not need to converse; before talking, he knows what the other wishes to say. The condition of the person or persons before him is revealed; it is like reading a letter. The person may speak to him, but without listening he knows. This is not thought reading, not telepathy, not psychometry or clairvoyance as people think. Revelation is all the phenomena there are. What is it? It is a fuller development of inspiration. When the intuitive faculty is fully developed, man receives revelation. All dumb creatures and mute things begin to speak. For what are words? Are they not covers over ideas? No feeling can ever be expressed in words; no idea can be put fully into verse. A true glimpse of ideas and feelings can only be perceived in that plane which is feeling itself.

One may ask, how does one arrive at this revelation? The answer is that there is nothing in the whole of the universe which is not to be found in man, if he only cares to discover it.

But if he will not find it, no one will give it to him. For truth is not learned; truth is discovered.

It was with this belief that the sages of the East went into solitude and sat meditating in order to give revelation an opportunity to arise. No doubt as life is at present there is hardly time for a man to go into solitude, but that does not mean that he should remain ignorant of the best that is within himself; for compared with this great bliss which is revelation, all other treasures of the earth are nothing. Revelation is the magic lamp of Aladdin. Once discovered it throws its light to the right and to the left, and all things become clear.

Revelation depends upon purity of mind. Very often someone who is worldly-wise is not really wise. Intellectuality is one thing; wisdom is another thing. Not all the knowledge learned from books and from experiences in the world and collected in the mind as learning is wisdom. When the light from within is thrown upon this knowledge, then the knowledge from outer life and the light coming from within make perfect wisdom; and it is that wisdom which guides man on the path of life.

Those who received revelation have given us sacred books such as the Bible, the Qur'an, and the Bhagavad Gita. Hundreds and thousands of years have passed, and their sacred teachings remain alive even now. But at the same time we must know that what they gave in the form of preaching, in the form of teachings is the interpretation of the living wisdom which cannot be fully expressed in words. One can only know that living knowledge when one has experienced it oneself by the opening of the heart. It is then that the purpose of life is fulfilled.

Index

Abraham, 223
accomplishment, 40f, 72, 96, 161, 167, 218, 227
action, 11, 19, 20f, 117, 162, 165, 169, 189
activity, 86, 112f, 126, 214, 231
aina khana, 58
air, 29, 97, 199
akasha, 9
Akbar, 193
Aladdin, 233
alchemy, 5ff, 192
Amina, 224
Amir, 70
analysis, 5, 195
anarchists, 65
anger, 12f
animals, 56, 58-63, 102, 172, 196, 207
art, 53, 122, 189, 208, 230
Asaf, 71
asceticism, 53
astral, 221, 223
atman, 131
atmosphere, 169ff, 185

atoms, 109f, 179, 217
attainment, 146, 160, 183
attitude, 43, 77, 138-144, 152, 178
attribute, 111
attunement, 27
autosuggestion, 55
Ayaz, 42f

balance, 89, 105, 141, 160, 175, 194, 196
beauty, 19ff, 31, 35, 53, 77, 142f
beckoning, 50
belief, 43ff, 146
Bhagavad Gita, 233
Bible, 10, 45, 101, 184, 217, 224, 233
blame, 32ff
blessing(s), 54, 67, 99
bodhisattva, 77, 79
body, 8-9, 18, 28, 95, 102, 104, 108, 124ff, 133f, 156, 165, 172f, 183, 193. *See also* mind and _____

Brahma, 122
Brahmans, 18
brain, 8, 28f, 66, 82ff, 86
breath, 108, 129-138, 165f, 170f, 186
Buddha, Gautama, 11, 128

character, 52, 162, 180, 197
children, 39f, 45, 79
Christ, Jesus, 11, 79, 89ff, 136, 175, 224
cobra, 135ff, 177
color(s), 29, 37f
communication, 31, 59, 63-67, 92, 108f
concentration, 9, 34, 62, 73, 85, 98, 102, 105-123, 127, 149-50, 164f, 168, 174, 178, 187, 204ff, 213, 222, 227, 229
-automatic and intentional, 106f
-kinds of, 111, 119f
-and love, 118ff
-and mind, 62, 98, 164, 174, 205
-mystical, 109-123
-stages of, 113
-ways to achieve, 106ff, 110
-and will, 96, 110, 164
conscience, 38f
consciousness, 30, 96f, 109, 147, 184, 225
contemplation, 104f, 107f
contentment, 140f, 162
control, 52, 101, 113, 127, 161, 179

creation, 10-15, 73, 85, 96f, 114, 121f, 159, 165, 177, 200, 223
creativity, 73f, 89, 205f
crucifixion, 104, 162

Daniel, 60
dead, 65f
death, 49, 60, 84, 104, 134, 155f, 177, 215f, 231
dervishes, 51
Desdemona, 34
desire(s), 70, 101
destruction, 53f, 85, 89, 159
devotion, 89, 110, 120, 223, 227
discipline, 77, 99, 102, 137f
dishonesty, 152f
djinns, 217, 225
dream(s), 31, 112, 122, 200, 213-221, 224ff

earth, 10, 29, 75, 89, 97f, 199
echo, 20
education, 79
ego, 102, 191
elements, the, 29f, 97, 199
elephant(s), 60f, 226
endurance, 91f
enthusiasm, 141
esotericism, 3-7, 85
ether, 29, 199
evil, 16, 19, 32, 75
expression, 192-201
extension, 173
eyes, 131f, 167f, 172, 174, 180ff, 196ff, 205

face, 194, 196-197

failure, 72f, 96, 152f, 159, 187

fana-fi-shaikh, 227

fancy, 162

fear, 122

feeling(s), 7, 9, 14f, 49, 88-92, 103, 133, 165, 179, 184, 194, 203f, 232. *See also* heart

feet, 80, 169

Firdawsi, 224

fire, 29, 97, 161, 163, 199

foresight, 174

forgiveness, 70, 90

form(s), 30f, 37, 155f, 195-196

food, 134, 166

freedom, 67, 98f, 191

Gabriel, 223

gain and loss, 160

glance, 168, 177, 182, 184

God, 16, 19, 21, 26, 44f, 77, 92, 96f, 104, 121, 129, 133f, 148f, 162, 167, 175, 211, 222ff
-belief in, 26, 146
-communication with, 229ff
-concentration on, 121, 176
-as Creator, 11f, 95f, 122, 196, 200, 223
-knowledge of, 109, 195
-love of, 26, 92, 96, 195
-and man, 41, 48, 89f, 100, 122f, 133f, 193, 223
-power of, 95, 163
-presence of, 193
-realization of, 26, 147ff, 184
-and will, 96f, 103f, 123, 162

goodness, 16, 19f, 75, 90f, 143f, 152

gusha nashini, 116

Hafiz, 114

hand, 169

happiness, 20, 83

hate, 41, 70

head, 195

healing, 12, 105ff, 118, 124, 129, 149, 159, 161, 166, 168ff

heart, 15, 63f, 68, 69-74, 88-92, 97, 121, 133, 180ff, 194f, 203, 207, 211, 225f, 233

heaven, 10f, 75, 83, 85, 90, 155, 183, 231

hell, 11, 83, 155

Hindu(s), 16, 20, 112, 122, 165, 223

honesty, 152f

hope, 43, 140

horse(s), 59, 62f, 98

humility, 138f

ideal, 99

imagination, 9, 25-31, 122, 203ff, 213, 215

iman, 177

imperfection, 143

impression(s), 37-43, 66, 68, 82, 115, 142f, 185-201, 202f, 217, 230

impulse, 19, 77, 96, 203

independence, 186

indifference, 186

individual, 17f, 156

inner world, 105, 131, 183f, 192, 208, 222, 224ff, 232f

insects, 58, 62

insight, 52, 162, 172-184, 193, 231

inspiration, 153, 164, 184, 207-212, 230

intellect, 89f, 200, 233

intelligence, 29, 84, 99, 112, 136, 204, 226, 231

interest, 178

intuition, 114, 184, 194f, 198, 202-206, 226, 230

Jamshyd, 223, 225

Jilani, Abdal Qader, 163

Joseph, 223

judgment, 79

Judgment Day, 69

justice, 20, 34

kadr, 104

kalpa vraksha, 14

kashf, 194

kaza, 104

kemal, 115

Khamush, 182

Khidr, 77ff

khilvat, 116

Khuda, 230

khwabi ghalti, 218f

khwabi khayali, 218

kismet, 13

knowledge, 4, 84, 144, 175, 206, 211, 230, 233

Kounsa, 51

Krishna, 51, 128

language, 47f, 50, 59, 61

law, 19, 84, 215

laziness, 102f

learning, 145f

life, 49, 53, 99f, 115ff, 138ff, 155, 169ff, 175, 177, 194, 208f

light, 70, 97, 154, 169, 195, 204, 229, 233

limitation(s), 44, 71f

lions, 60

love, 41, 70, 89ff, 96, 118ff, 195. *See also* heart

Mahadeva, 51

majdhub, 167

man, 16f, 58-63, 91f, 95f, 174. *See also* God and ___

manas, 16

mantra shastra, 67

mantra yoga, 45, 48f

manu, manushi, 16

Mary, the Virgin, 224

Masnavi, the, 97

master mind(s), 184, 206

mastery, 35, 73, 85, 115f, 117f, 122, 127, 144, 164, 190, 227

matter, 4

mechanism, 97

meditation, 85, 104, 108f, 130, 148ff, 164, 222, 227

memory, 9, 82-87, 112, 154f

mind, 27, 76, 80, 111, 155f, 161f, 174, 193f, 202, 215f
-of animals, 58ff
-and attitude, 138-144
-and body, 8-9, 84, 125ff, 131, 133f, 149, 164ff, 173, 175f, 179, 188, 214f, 217
-and breath, 129-138
-clarity of, 28, 30f, 58, 63, 67, 73, 129
-condition of, 63f, 114f, 196f, 204f
-control of, 85f, 98, 102f, 127, 164, 205f, 213
-creation of, 10-15, 30
-divine, 16-21, 87, 207f, 211
-and dream, 213-222
-and heart, 64, 88, 133, 183, 203
-impressions on, 187ff, 214, 222
-of the mystic, 17ff
-nature of, 8-9, 17f, 23-92 passim, 164, 215
-power of, 62, 67, 119, 125f, 165
-purification of, 124-144
-purity of, 151-156, 233
-of the seer, 157-233 passim
-and soul, 134, 173, 183, 221f, 230
-stilling of, 124-129, 166, 204
-subconscious, 30, 154f
-training of, 93-156 passim, 216
-tranquility of, 101, 129, 166, 187, 227
-working of, 27ff, 36, 126f

miraj, 224

mirror(s), 64, 70, 73, 89

modesty, 41ff

Moghul, 51

Moses, 77ff, 223, 229

motive, 30, 99f, 118, 167

movement(s), 49-54, 197, 198-200

Muhammad, 224

mureed, 121, 163

murshid, 44, 77ff, 121, 169, 209

music, 46f, 53, 61f, 82f, 136, 189f

Muslim, 20

mystic(s), 17ff, 40, 49, 58, 77, 115f, 118f, 128, 136f, 173, 193f

mysticism, 4, 7, 13, 131

nafs, 131

names, 39f, 111

Napoleon, 40

nature, 121f, 159, 230

object(s), 56, 112f, 161, 185f, 223

observation, 111f, 174f, 197

obsession, 65-67

offering, 65

Omar Khayyam, 10

omens, 37f
oneness, 17f, 69
openness, 178
opinion, 33f, 36, 188
optimism, 97, 139f
Othello, 34

Paderewski, Ignace, 106
pain, 38, 61, 99, 118f, 147
past, 72, 189, 192, 220, 222f
patience, 91, 149
peace, 179
penetration, 172f, 177
perfection, 21, 45, 118, 143, 167
pessimism, 97f, 139f
phenomena, 151
pleasure, 118f, 147
possessions, 13
posture(s), 125, 130, 138
power, 14, 95, 100, 123, 159ff, 163f. *See also* psychic power; will power
praise, 32ff
prayer, 122, 130
pride, 138f
prophet(s), 77, 208, 224f
psychic power, 159-171, 175
psychology, 3-7, 33, 41, 49, 192
purification, mental, 124-144, 146ff
purity, 151-156, 173, 187, 233
purpose (of life), 85, 91, 109, 120, 127, 233

Qur'an, 19, 60, 69, 97, 197, 200, 224, 233

rajas, 77
Rama, 223
rasul, 121, 225
realization, 19, 89, 104, 109, 137, 146
reason, 9, 75-81, 174
receptivity, 65, 79, 202, 206
record, 82ff, 108, 187-192
reflection, 17, 29, 31, 58-74
religion(s), 15, 146, 223
repetition, 45, 48f, 67-69
repose, 86, 112f, 125, 136, 166
resignation, 104, 140, 162
result, 162
resurrection, 104
revelation, 184, 229-233
Revelations, 224
rhythm, 80, 86, 179, 186, 231
Rumi, Jalal ad-din, 97, 128

Sa'adi, 137, 197, 232
safa, 173
sahib-e dil, 184
salutations, 50
Sanskrit, 11, 16, 122, 138
sati, 83
sattva, 77
science, 3-7, 130ff. 207. 230
scriptures, 15. *See also* Bhagavad Gita; Bible; Qur'an; Vedas
seclusion, 116, 179, 233

seeing, 7, 174ff, 181
seer, 7, 77, 157-233 passim
self-confidence, 177
self-consciousness, 113, 227f
self-control, 53, 194
self-denial, 101
self-discipline, 99
selfishness, 160
self-sacrifice, 91
sensation, 105
senses, 29, 82, 154, 190
Shiva, 135, 165, 177, 190
sin, 11
single-mindedness, 116f
sleep, 72, 127f, 213-221 passim
snake(s), 61f. *See also* cobra
Solomon, 16, 70, 223
soul, 96, 109, 128, 131ff, 154, 172ff, 176, 180, 184, 221, 229
spirit, 4, 11, 48, 66, 156, 174, 207f, 211
steadiness, 165f, 168
success, 72f, 96, 152f, 159, 172, 187
Sufi(s), 20, 51, 58, 89, 118, 128, 137, 173, 194
  -path of, 85, 91, 120
  -practices of, 48, 67f, 73, 85, 101f, 112, 116f, 182, 227
  -teachings of, 104, 115, 121, 149
Sufism, 176
suggestion, 32-57, 161
Sungam, 19

symbolism, 216, 220-221, 223ff
synthesis, 5, 195

Taj Mahal, 96
tamas, 77
tasawwur, 121, 149, 227
taste, 190
thinking, 25f, 28, 214
third eye, 180
thought(s), 11, 13f, 25-31, 64, 67f, 73, 77, 98, 164f, 187f, 194, 204
tone, 46f, 186
tranquility, 101, 166, 179, 211
trimurti, 175
truth, 26, 183, 233

unlearning, 145-150
uruj, 115

vairagya, 186
Vajad Ali Shah, 51
Valmiki, 223
Vedanta, 176, 179
Vedas, 16
vibration(s), 97, 109, 185, 197, 217
viprit karnai, 190
virtue, 11f, 19f
vision(s), 114, 181, 184, 222-228
visionary, 29, 226f
visualization, 111
voice, 45-49, 130

water, 29, 44, 89, 97, 100, 129, 134, 151, 166f, 199

wazifa, 67

will, 27, 63, 95-104, 110, 112, 154, 179, 181, 213

will power, 14, 62f, 86, 95-104, 164, 179

wisdom, 100f, 146, 152, 160ff, 175, 206, 211, 231, 233

word(s), 45-49, 168

yogi(s), 48, 91, 116, 135, 177, 182

zaval, 115

Zoroaster, 11